Single With A Goal

Relationship Readiness

Single With A Goal
Relationship Readiness

Copyright © 2025 by A Champion's Heart Inc. | Family Success Solutions

All rights reserved.

No part of this book may be reproduced, stored in a retrieval system, or transmitted in any form or by any means—electronic, mechanical, photocopying, recording, or otherwise—without the prior written permission of the publisher, except for brief quotations used in critical articles or reviews.

Published in Pennsauken, New Jersey

by A Champion's Heart Inc. | Family Success Solutions

www.achampsheart.com

Scripture References:Unless otherwise noted, all Scripture quotations are taken from the King James Version (KJV), the Amplified Bible (AMP), and the English Standard Version (ESV).

All rights to quoted translations remain with their respective copyright holders.

This book is a work of empowerment, transformation, and spiritual education. The stories, principles, and teachings herein reflect the lived experience, biblical understanding, and clinical insight of the author and are intended to inspire, equip, and renew the minds of its readers.

ISBN: 979-8-9999035-0-1

Printed in the United States of America

Single With A Goal

Relationship Readiness

Transforming Your Mind
Preparing Your Heart
Building Your Relationship Future

By Coach Will Lane

A Champion's Heart Inc. | Family Success Solution

Dedication

To my incredible wife, Tangela — my partner, my friend, my prayer warrior, and the captain of my personal cheer squad (lol). Your love, grace, belief, and patience have strengthened me in ways I can never fully express. Thank you for believing in our call and mission to transform and heal families.
Thank you for standing with me.

To my children, Will Jr., Kayla, and Faith — you are my legacy. Every lesson I teach, I teach first for you. May you grow to build relationships, marriage, and families that reflect God's love, anchored in truth, healed, whole, with abundant happiness, and fun. Dad loves you.

To my mentor, Dr. James D. Treadwell Jr., and your amazing wife Deana Treadwell — thank you for modeling a God-centered marriage, for believing in me, and for pouring your wisdom into my life. Your faithfulness has inspired me to pursue wholeness and purpose in my own family and to help others do the same.

Contents

Foreward

Acknowledgments

Preface

Introduction

Relationship Attachment Self-Check

(page 1)
Chapter 1: Single With A Goal
Reframing singleness as preparation, not punishment

(page 13)
Chapter 2: Renewing My Relationship Blueprint
Breaking free from family patterns and building on God's truth

(page 27)
Chapter 3: The Culture vs. The Kingdom
Exchanging worldly dating mindsets for Kingdom values

CONTENTS

(page 43)
Chapter 4: Identity — Wholeness Before Oneness
Finding confidence and security in Christ before seeking a partner

(page 57)
Chapter 5: Purpose Over Preference
Redefining "your type" through healing and mission alignment

(page 69)
Chapter 6: Redefining Love: Commitment, Sacrifice & Covenant
Moving beyond feelings to build a covenant foundation

(page 81)
Chapter 7: Boundaries, Purity, and Honor
Protecting yourself and honoring God in your relationship choices

(page 95)
Chapter 8: Healing Father & Mother Wounds
Breaking generational cycles and building emotional health

CONTENTS

(page 107)

<u>Chapter 9: The Power of Accountability and Community</u>

Building a Godly support network to stay on track

(page 119)

<u>Chapter 10: God's Timing vs. Your Timeline</u>

Trusting God's perfect timing and resisting the rush

(page 131)

<u>Chapter 11: Discerning the Right Relationship</u>

Using biblical wisdom to test character and compatibility

(page 145)

<u>Chapter 12: Becoming Marriage Ready Whole, Healed & Anchored</u>

Bringing it all together for a purposeful, God-honoring relationship

Closing Prayer
Call To Action
Relationship Affirmation Decree Vault
About the Author
Recommended Resources

Foreword

In a world where the very foundation of relationships—particularly marriage—is under increasing strain, clarity, truth, and preparation have never been more essential. We live in a time when many enter into covenant relationships without the necessary understanding, healing, or personal wholeness required to sustain them. That is why this book is not just timely—it is vital.

Relationship Readiness Before You Get Married is more than a self-help guide. It is a transformational tool and a spiritual training ground for anyone who dares to look inward before stepping into lifelong partnership. In these pages, Will Lane walks the reader through a journey of self-awareness, intentional growth, and heart-level transformation. He addresses the mindsets, belief systems, and personal patterns that often go unchecked but can derail a relationship before it ever truly begins.

I have had the privilege of knowing Will Lane for many years. He is not only a committed son in the faith but a loyal protégé, one whose life is a reflection of the principles he teaches. His passion for truth, wholeness, and healthy covenant is evident in every word he writes. He doesn't just talk about transformation—he embodies it.

Whether you're a single person preparing for marriage, a counselor or mentor guiding others, or an educator helping shape future generations, this book has something to offer you. It speaks to the individual heart, yet its message is powerful enough to shift culture. It challenges us to make personal transformation a priority—not just for the sake of a future spouse, but for the sake of our own God-given destiny.

Read this book with an open heart. Let it examine you, stretch you, and call you higher. And may it prepare you—not just for marriage, but for a life of purpose, wholeness, and lasting impact.

—Dr. James David Treadwell Jr

August 2025

Acknowledgments

First and foremost, I give thanks to God, my "Good-Good Father", Jesus— my Redeemer and Hero, and Holy Spirit my helper and "plus One". By you I received the strength, wisdom, and vision to write this book and walk this path of healing and transformation and destroying the works of the enemy regarding family.

To my mentor, **Dr. James D. Treadwell Jr., and his wife, Deana Treadwell** — your consistent faith, your example of a godly marriage, and your relentless investment in my growth have changed my life. Thank you for teaching and training me to think higher, love deeper, and trust God in genuine faith without a contingency plan.

Your work, "I Am a Soul Man", has ingrained in me that all prosperity and health in life is dependent upon the condition of my SOUL -mind, will & emotions (3John 2). You have instilled in me that there can be absolutely no transformation in any aspect of life without mind renewal (Romans 12:2). You are a true reformer with a legacy of transformation

Acknowledgements

and fearlessness to confront some of the most challenging" subjects head on. You have reproduced that into me. Now I am paying it forward. As a kid, I heard you sing your heart song- "If I can help somebody..." Now, over 40 years later, we are singing that song as a real-life duet.

To my incredible wife, Tangela — your love, prayers, patience, and encouragement have been the glue that holds me steady. You have shown me what covenant looks like in action, and I am forever grateful for you. Together, we lived this book over 30 years ago prior to marriage and still continue to be the living version of it today.

Thank you — "HoneyGirl"

To my extended family, close friends, Gatekeepers Kingdom Impact Ministries Community. You undergird as a support system. It is within this community that I have partaken of over 250 cumulative years of Happy, Healthy, Fulfilling Marriages. Thank you for believing in me, challenging me, and reminding me that iron sharpens iron.

Acknowledgements

To every single reader who trusts me with their story, and dares to believe that transformation is possible, and who is ready to break cycles and build something new —I am honored to serve you. You are the reason this book exists.

I want to extend deep gratitude to my spiritual grandfather in the faith, **Dr. Bill Hamon**, whose work "Who Am I and Why Am I Here?" has deeply impacted my life and understanding of God's design for identity, purpose, and family. His teachings remind us that, "God created the family as the foundational training ground for fulfilling His purpose on earth."

Bishop, your revelation has helped me and countless others realize that healing our hearts and aligning with God's intention for relationships is not just about personal wholeness — it's about divine assignment.

Acknowledgements

Thank you, Bishop Hamon, for teaching generations how to walk in purpose, live prophetically, and honor the original blueprint of God's heart for family. You have reproduced yourself into my mentor and spiritual father, Dr. James D. Treadwell Jr. and he has no doubt reproduced himself into me. As you say, "We are reproducers, of reproducers, who reproduce, reproducers...."

Preface

From the bottom of my heart, I want to welcome you on this journey. Whether you picked up this book because you're frustrated with dating, afraid of repeating your parents' mistakes, longing for a godly marriage, or just curious about what "relationship readiness" really means.

I want you to know this: you are in the right place.
I didn't write this book from a place of theory, but from real life — from challenges and breakthroughs, from failures and victories, from moments when I wondered if I could ever build a healthy relationship, and from decades of watching God transform not just my own marriage, but the marriages and families of those I've served and those with whom I have served with.

I believe with everything in me that healing, growth, and purpose are possible — no matter where you start. God specializes in taking what's broken and making it whole. But that change doesn't happen by accident; it happens on purpose, with intentional choices and a renewed mind.

This book is an invitation to do just that: to renew your mind, confront your patterns, and prepare your heart for a relationship that honors God. It is not a quick fix or a checklist — it is a roadmap for transformation, one chapter at a time.

Along the way, you will be challenged. You will be stretched. You may even have to lay down beliefs you've carried your whole life.

But I promise you — if you lean in, do the work, and trust God through every page, you will walk away more whole, more healed, and more ready than ever to build a purposeful, lasting relationship.

I'm so grateful to walk this path with you.

Let's build from the inside out — together.

Introduction

Family, welcome!
You didn't pick up this book by accident. Deep down, you know there's more to love and relationships than what you've seen, what you've been taught, or what you've lived so far. Maybe you're tired of failed dating patterns. Maybe you've watched generational cycles repeat. Maybe you've been told to "just wait for the right one" without ever being taught how to become the right one.

The Goal is to do relationship and marriage God's way and this book is your fresh start. You're about to take a powerful, transformational journey — one that will challenge your thinking, confront your wounds, renew your mindset, and position you to build a healthy, purpose-driven relationship from the inside out.

Introduction

Understand this: I'm not here to offer you a dating checklist, or a quick fix, or "ten steps to catching a spouse." I'm here to invite you into something much bigger. This book is about becoming. Becoming healed. Becoming whole. It's about becoming wise and anchored in God's truth.

I believe with all my heart that marriage is one of God's greatest gifts — but only if you're prepared for it. Without preparation, marriage can expose and multiply your brokenness. But with preparation, it can be a force for healing, restoration, and generational change.

Each chapter of this book is designed to help you break free from toxic patterns, challenge cultural confusion, and walk in purpose and identity. You will see how to:

- Recognize where your patterns came from
- Rebuild your mindset around biblical truth
- Honor God through boundaries and purity
- Heal from family wounds
- Trust God's timing
- Discern the right relationship
- And ultimately, stand ready for a marriage that brings God glory

Introduction

I made a conscious decision to leave out chapters and pages of statistics and quantitative studies from my years of family dynamics research, training, and experience because I know that you're genuinely looking for: solutions to your problem. You didn't pick up this book for a lecture. You picked it up because you're ready for transformation.

This is not about me flaunting my accumulated knowledge or quoting facts that only serve to impress. For example, a 2023 survey revealed that approximately 40% of married Americans have regrets about their marriage, and 1 in 10 report those regrets on their wedding day. Those are serious numbers — but let's be honest—knowing those statistics won't protect you from becoming one of them. Because knowledge alone doesn't bring change.

> With all sincerity, I say this: "Without wisdom and understanding anchored in the Word of God, knowledge can leave you arrogant and puffed up , but still confused and hurting. You'll become a smart person who is still clueless when it comes to building a healthy, lasting relationship. (1 Corinthians 8:1-3)"

Introduction

Family, transformation doesn't happen through information. Transformation happens through mind renewal (Romans 12:2). This book was written as a tool and a blueprint, to help you exchange limiting beliefs, toxic patterns, and cultural conditioning that sabotages relationships and the marriage covenant for God-breathed truth.

Therefore, my approach throughout this entire book is to coach you, prompt you, and provoke you into the good work of mind renewal. This is the kind of renewal that changes how you think, how you love, and how you show up. And when that happens? Everything changes. Your relationships, your marriage, your family, and your legacy will benefit.

I'm going to be honest with you — this won't always feel comfortable. Some pages might confront you. Some chapters might make you pause and reflect more deeply than you ever have. But that's exactly where transformation happens. If you lean in, do the work, pray through each chapter, and let the Holy Spirit guide you, you will not be the same person by the final page. You will be more confident, more healed, more purposeful, and more prepared to build a relationship that reflects God's love.

Introduction

I'm here to walk this journey with you. So grab your Bible, grab your S.W.A.G. Workbook journal and let's get started.

It's time to build your relatiohships from the inside out.

— *Coach Will*

Attachment Style Self-Check

Before you begin Chapter 1, let's pause for a moment of powerful self-reflection.

Most of us have never been taught how we attach to others in the manner that we do, whether that's in dating, friendships, family, or even Church communities. Our past experiences, family history, and even our culture shape the ways we connect, trust, and open up. Understanding your attachment style is a tool—not a label. It gives you a mirror — a chance to see where you may need healing, growth, and mind renewal as you step into the Kingdom principles taught throughout this book.

WHY UNDERSTANDING YOUR ATTACHMENT STYLE MATTERS

- You cannot change what you don't recognize

- Knowing your patterns helps you break them

- Your attachment tendencies influence all relationships, not just romantic ones

- Bringing them to light gives you the power to renew your mind with intention

- God's truth can transform any relational blueprint

Expect to heal, grow in your secure attachment style through God's truth and love

● ● ● ● ● ● ● ●

Instructions

Check the box underneath your answer.				
1 Never	2 Rarely	3 Sometimes	4 Often	5 Always

12-Question Mini Attachment Self-Check

1. I worry that people I care about will abandon me.

1 Never	2 Rarely	3 Sometimes	4 Often	5 Always

2. I often felt like I'm too much for others to handle.

1 Never	2 Rarely	3 Sometimes	4 Often	5 Always

3. When conflicts happen, I tend to pull away or isolate myself.

1 Never	2 Rarely	3 Sometimes	4 Often	5 Always

4. I often look for reassurance that I'm valued or loved.

1 Never	2 Rarely	3 Sometimes	4 Often	5 Always

5. I find it hard to fully trust people's motives.

1	2	3	4	5
Never	Rarely	Sometimes	Often	Always

6. I'm uncomfortable sharing my deepest fears and/or struggles.

1	2	3	4	5
Never	Rarely	Sometimes	Often	Always

7. I believe if I don't please people, they may leave me or stop caring.

1	2	3	4	5
Never	Rarely	Sometimes	Often	Always

8. I sometimes feel possessive about people who are important to me.

1	2	3	4	5
Never	Rarely	Sometimes	Often	Always

9. I avoid getting too close so I won't be disappointed.

1 Never	2 Rarely	3 Sometimes	4 Often	5 Always

10. I feel nervous when people I care about pull back, go quiet, or seem distant.

1 Never	2 Rarely	3 Sometimes	4 Often	5 Always

11. I struggle to rely on others for support when I need help.

1 Never	2 Rarely	3 Sometimes	4 Often	5 Always

12. I feel torn between wanting emotional closeness and needing time to myself.

1 Never	2 Rarely	3 Sometimes	4 Often	5 Always

Enter Your Total Score

Scoring Key & Style Descriptions

12-24: You lean toward a secure attachment style. You generally believe you are worthy of love and connection, and you can trust others while maintaining your independence.

25-39: You show patterns of anxious or preoccupied attachment. You might fear rejection, seek constant reassurance, or worry about people leaving.

40-60: You may lean toward an avoidant or fearful attachment. You might hold back, avoid closeness, or struggle to trust because of past hurts or fear of losing your sense of control.

Bible Based Framing

Family, your score is not a life sentence. It is simply a snapshot of where you are today — and a glimpse at possible trouble areas caused by conditioning that God can transform as you renew your mind.

> **"Be transformed by the renewing of your mind" (Romans 12:2)**

You will grow, heal, and learn secure, God-centered ways to love and connect. — through community, prayer, biblical truth, and intentional personal development.

Remember:
- *This book is not intended to be just informational; It is a transformational journey.*
- *Your attachment patterns can be renewed through God's truth and healing.*
- *You are worthy of secure, healthy love — from God, and through godly relationships.*

Chapter 1

Single With A Goal

"Being Single is Not a Punishment It's Preparation"

Have you ever sat at a wedding reception, watching the bride and groom spin across the dance floor, while you sat in the back, wondering when it would be your turn? Or how about being the happily supportive cheerleader of friends, colleagues, and family as they are seemingly one by one being swept away by "their one". Or maybe you've scrolled social media late at night, seeing random strangers get engaged, married, or start families, and you felt a wave of fear wash over you, as if you were somehow falling behind or left out.

Let me tell you — you're not behind and you haven't been left out.

The world has tried to convince us that being single is some kind of punishment or failure.

It tries to convince us that if you're not paired up, you're incomplete. That if you're alone, you're missing out. **But let me say this plainly:**

> *"Singleness is not Punishishment It is Preparation"*

I know that experience first hand because I had to live it. I grew up in a single-parent home. I saw the heartbreak and disappointment, the struggle to fulfill dual roles, the dysfunction that comes from trying to build a relationship on a broken foundation. I made myself a promise early on that I wouldn't repeat those mistakes. I committed to myself that I'd never let my future family experience the same kind of pain and insecurity I witnessed.

But deep down, I was scared — scared I might turn out just like the men before me that lived with infidelity, abuse, and divorce. That jolted me and made me desperate to get it right. Despite not having a model of what right was. It made me want to rush into relationships. It made me want to grab hold of marriage before I was truly ready, before I was whole. I almost gave my future away just to fill my present loneliness.

But God had a different plan.

He slowed me down. He put a person in my life — a coach, a pastor, and a mentor — who showed me the power of mind renewal. He revealed to me that there can be no transformation without renewing your mind, and there can be no healthy relationship until you are healed, whole, and rooted in HIM. Through my mentor, Dr. James D. Treadwell jr., God taught me that singleness was a gift. It was my season to become. To become the man He designed me to be. To build character, to heal wounds, to grow my spiritual maturity, so I could one day lead and love well in marriage. This also came with a community of men who would model the

"There can be no Transformation with out Mind Renewal"

same lessons that I was learning. I was then blessed to rub shoulders with others who had successfully used their single season as their time to grow, mature, and develop as a whole individual and were now enjoying the fruits of their personal development within their relationships.

That season was stretching and often uncomfortable. But it was the best thing that ever happened to me.

Cultural Conditioning

But just Look around. Culture wants you to believe the opposite, as it works to condition us to believe, think, and experience its lies. Culture says:

- "You're worthless if you're alone."
- "You'll be alone if you don't lower your standards and moral values.
- "Just hook up and move on."
- "If you wait too long, you'll miss your chance."
- "Guys, if you don't have multiple sexual partners, you are weak, "wack", or lame."
- "Ladies, it's old-fashioned to preserve yourself until marriage.

Unfortunately, there are too many more to list here. This is the culture's method to pressure you into its perspectives by succumbing to the "Culture Cookie Cutter."

The Culture Cookie Cutter

Romans 12:2 gives us a command, not a suggestion: "Be not conformed to this world, but be transformed by the renewing of your mind." The word "conformed" carries a powerful warning because the urge to conform is frequently driven by social pressure, both overt and subtle.

You will tend to yield to this pressure when there is the fear of rejection, and the desire to be accepted, liked, and affirmed by the culture.

This pressurized conformity paints a picture of you being forced into a mold. I like to illustrate it this way: culture acts like a cookie cutter as it presses down with force, trying to shape your identity, beliefs, and relationships to fit its agenda. It wants to pressure you into sameness, to mold your mindset according to trends, lies, and superficial values. But Romans 12:2 says resist it. Do not allow the world to press you into its shape and design. Instead, God calls us to transformation, not through pressure, but through mind renewal. Renewal changes us from the inside out. Where culture pushes, God invites. Where culture molds, God transforms. And that transformation begins in your mind.

> **"Do not allow the world to press you into its shape and design."**

Because culture rejects this, sadly, I must ask how many of those relationships we celebrated ended up broken, miserable, or repeating the same generational cycles? The answer: Too many! In my opinion, one instance is too many because there are hearts, futures, young minds, and generational consequences at stake.

Think on this

Things don't just go bad — they start bad.
When a building collapses, the problem is rarely in the walls you see. It's usually an issue within the foundation, you don't see. Friend, your singleness is not a punishment; it is meant to be a time of preparation and your opportunity to build your foundation right.

Preparation is God's way to bring the best out of us. In fact, it's his process for all of creation. We are no exception. Plant organs, especially roots, experience positive gravitropic growth as they extend downward in cooperation with gravity's pull. This process is crucial for the quality of plant development, which ensures roots grow downwards into the soil for anchorage and nutrient absorption. Downward or "inward growth" is paramount to lasting success.

Likewise, the gestation period is a living, biological illustration of God's principle: To Gestate means to conceive and carry in the womb for development until birth. He prepares, He develops and He forms in stages, He protects, He reveals at the proper time (Jeremiah 1:5). Just as the conceived human being requires this period of careful development in the womb before birth, we witness this same personal development "gestation period" in the lives of some of our favorite athletes, artists, entrepreneurs, first responders, and more. Because the wise person understands that to "gestate" also means to conceive and gradually develop in the mind for the purpose of reflection, renewal, subsequent growth, and transformation.

My friend, you need this season of intentional personal growth and healing before stepping into a relationship. Rushing into relationships without this preparatory "gestation" can lead to unhealthy patterns but allowing God to shape and develop you fully prepares you for a healthy, purpose-filled partnership. God says in Ephesians 2:10 that you were created in Christ for good works, which He prepared in advance for you to walk in.

That means that your season of singleness is no accident. It is an assignment that prepares you for your mission. Jesus prepared for thirty years for his mission as Savior of the World. Paul, the Apostle, spent 14 years in the desert being prepared by God, not including the years of tutelage under masters of the Mosaic law. Please understand that the duration of time spent in preparation is not the main point here. The condition of your heart that is evidenced by openness to learn, reflect, renew the mind, and become the transformed you is.

As a lifelong athlete, I have often reflected on my attitude about the "off-season".

This is a quiet time with no cheering. No fans, no tackles or interceptions to be made, or touchdowns to be scored in comparison to the actual game. However, it is a time for investment, because the level of investment you put into your "task-specific" off-season training determines your return during the season. My friend, I know firsthand that a "task-specific", proactive approach to preparation pays off. Michael Jordan, often considered to be the best Basketball player of all time said, "Some people want it to happen, some wish it would happen, and others make it happen." This was a statement he made regarding his offseason training. You see, Michael Jordan could not "make it happen" during the season if he did not make his steady growth, development, mind-renewal, and player transformation happen in the offseason. This was his investment for what he desired on the court in the future upcoming season. Tom Brady, considered to be one of the best "quarterbacks" of all time, encouraged young athletes to embrace the challenges of off-season training, highlighting the discipline required to train when others are resting.

"The level of Investment put into your Task-Specific Training determines your Relationship Success"

Here's the point: Your single season is your time of task-specific preparation, while other singles are sleepwalking through this time, and not preparing for that God-sent marriage life that they wish for.

You are not just "waiting around," You are becoming. You are being prepared for the mission of marriage — and for the mission of life.

Do This

- Write down three things you believe singleness has taught you so far.

1. _____

2. _____

3. _____

- Write one skill or mindset you now realize you need to grow in before you step into a relationship.

- _____
  _____
  _____

Journal This

- What does singleness mean to you right now?

- Who taught you your beliefs about being single?

- What is one cultural lie about singleness you need to break today?

- How can you use this season to invest in your personal growth?

—JOURNAL YOUR RESPONSE BELOW—

Chapter 1
BIG TAKEAWAY

> *"My singleness is a season of preparation & purpose. I am not behind. I am not being punished. I am being prepared."*

Transformational Affirmation Decrees for Your Season of Preparation

Family, listen — don't just read these affirmations like words on a page. Speak them with faith & intention. Let your heart agree with your mouth. Every time you declare truth, you're rewiring your thinking, breaking cultural lies, and partnering with God's vision for your life. These aren't hype — they're healing. Let's go!

1. I am whole, valuable, and complete in Christ in my season of singleness.
2. My single season is filled with purpose, preparation, and growth.
3. I choose to build a strong, godly foundation for my future.
4. I honor God with how I use this time to heal, mature, and develop.
5. I am being prepared for a purpose-filled relationship that reflects God's design.
6. I am right on time in God's plan for me.
7. I invest in my personal growth and allow God to shape my character.
8. I embrace God's perspective and reject the lies of culture.
9. I attract healthy relationships by becoming emotionally and spiritually whole.
10. I walk confidently in my identity, knowing God is writing my story with wisdom and love.

*"Family, you are not waiting for love — You are preparing for purpose.
Your singleness is not a setback; it is God's preparational setup for the relationship you are being shaped to steward.
So, choose to invest, grow, and become — because the foundation you lay now determines the future you will build later.
Be Whole, Be Healed, and Become
— on purpose."*

In Chapter 2, we're going to take an honest look at the relationship patterns you inherited — from your family, your past, and even your culture. It's time to lay those old blueprints on the table and ask a transforming question:

"Does this align with God's design?"

Get ready to confront, release, and replace what doesn't serve your purpose. Because your future relationship can only be as strong as the blueprint it's built on. **So, Let's go!**

Chapter 2

Renewing My Relationship Blueprint

"The inner scripts and beliefs you build relationships with will determine whether your castle stands or comes crashing down."

Have you ever stopped and asked yourself: "Why do I think about relationships the way I do?" Most of us never do. We just live out the patterns we were handed — from our family and community, our culture, or our past relationships. We build with those patterns as a foundation without really questioning them, until one day, those patterns collapse under the pressure of real life.

The truth is, no matter who you are — man or woman — you carry a relationship blueprint. Some of that blueprint is helpful. But some of it is downright toxic.

If you want to experience transformation in your relationships, you must be willing to renew the blueprint which requires renewing your mind about the blueprint you were given.

I grew up in a single-parent home, like a lot of people. Maybe you did, too. Or maybe you grew up with parents who stayed together, but fought constantly, or weaponized their silence. Maybe you saw cheating, manipulation, or fear. If we're honest, most of us didn't get a good blueprint handed to us. That means we have to pause, lay the old blueprint on the table, and ask God: "Is this what YOU want me to build my relationship life on?"

I remember telling myself I'd never end up like the men who abandoned their families. That seemed noble, right? But the fear behind that vow still shaped me. It made me guarded, overly obligated, falsely responsible, and afraid to trust.

Maybe for you, it's something else. Maybe you promised yourself you'd never depend on anyone, never get hurt again, you don't need a man, or that you'd always be the strong one in the relationship.

Sometimes those inner vows feel protective — but they become prisons. Because erecting a wall based on a past wound and attempting to keep out further harm will subsequently prevent that which is good for you from ever reaching you.

> *"A wall is a wall that has no regard for the reasons you erected it."*

Let's be real here: culture has been handing out faulty blueprints for generations; for instance.

Men are told to stay detached, dominant, and emotionally shut down.

Women are told to settle, to compete, and to perform for attention

Everyone in this culture is told to chase chemistry instead of commitment and covenant.

It's no wonder so many relationships are built on shaky ground. It's like building a house on the sand. Sooner or later, storms will come, and if your foundation is faulty, your relationship will collapse.

> ### Jesus said:
> "Whoever hears my words and puts them into practice is like a wise builder who built their house on the rock." (Matthew 7:24)

That's what this chapter is about — you becoming a wise relationship builder, no matter where and what you came from.

Mind Renewal is the Key

Renewing your blueprint requires doing an honest inventory. You must ask yourself tough questions like: What did I learn about love? What did I see modeled about trust? What do I believe about men, about women, about marriage? Do those beliefs line up with God's Word?

If they do, Awesome! But if they don't, it's time to trade them in. God's design for relationships is good, protective, and fulfilling — but let's be clear, it doesn't look anything like what we see in the world's culture.

Renewing the blueprint through replacement therapy

A huge part of renewing your mind is challenging the generalizations you might be carrying. Here are a few examples of culture's relationship generalizations:

- "All men are dogs."
- "There are no more good men left."
- "All women are out for something."
- "All women just want your money."

> **"All" is an absolute that is never true except as it pertains to God Himself"**

Family — These are just a few examples of the many lies that swirl around in the winds of culture. They are birthed from your bad experiences, and even from people who meant well but were wounded themselves.

Here's the truth: "All" is an absolute that is never true except as it pertains to God Himself. There are men who honor God, who are faithful, trustworthy, loving, and kind. There are women who are loyal, generous, virtuous, and sincere. Challenging and debunking the lies of culture requires you to be proactive and aggressive in order to keep a tight grip on God's perspective. You see, when culture swarms you with relationship opinions and arguments, the meaning you attach to what you hear and see from culture shapes your perspective. That meaning then gets place on the throne of your relationship belief system. It would sabotage all of your relationships, and cause you to repeat those same relationship patterns.

This is because the lies you believe become arguments in your mind that will always refute, fight, and combat the word of God. The same word of God that is your instruction manual for relationship success. ***You must make a decision to surrender your perspectives to the word of God.*** Be on the Word's side and use it as a weapon against culture's current. Use the bible as the filter and the scale for weighing your choices.

The lies and arguments you've believed — whether they came from family, heartbreak, trauma, or culture — don't just disappear because you start reading new scriptures. They often fight to dominate and intimidate like gang members in what my mentor, Dr. James D. Treadwell Jr., calls the neighborhood of the "SOUL." "Argument" as the gang affiliated partner of "Unbelief" is the gang spokes person in what I call "the courtroom of the soul."

Their activity , in your soul, that houses your mind, will, and emotions enables them to use culture's belief systems like legal evidence and arguments. And when God speaks truth into your life, your soul doesn't simply accept it. It Argues.
The argument may sound like:

—"I know what God says… but I've always been this way."
—"I can't trust anyone — I've been hurt too much."
—"This just feels unrealistic."

Those are not just thoughts. They're spiritual arguments that rise up to challenge the Word of God — and the danger is, if they go unchecked, they'll shape your relationships.That's why renewing your mind is spiritual warfare.

> **"Those are not just thoughts. They're spiritual arguments that rise up to challenge the Word of God"**

The Bible says in 2 Corinthians 10:4–5:

"The weapons of our warfare are not carnal but mighty through God for pulling down strongholds, casting down arguments and every high thing that exalts itself against the knowledge of God, and bringing every thought into captivity to the obedience of Christ."

When you believe something like "All men cheat" or "No woman can be trusted," that's not just pain or disappointment— that's an argument lodged in the soul. And it will combat the truth every time God tries to renew your blueprint. Family — this is the courtroom. You can't reason with an argument that's trying to overrule truth. You have to cast it down and speak God's Word louder. You must allow your mind to be renewed.

Here's what Dr. Treadwell taught me that I now teach you:

When you are "Born-again" our spirit agrees with God. Your soul must be renewed. If your soul is unrenewed, it will fight against your own healing. And until you shut down the arguments, you'll subconsciously sabotage the relationship you're praying for.

That's why we don't just read the Word — We WAR With It as a Weapon. In order to do so, the Word of God that you read must be Spoken out of your Mouth.

Declare this right now:

"I silence every argument in my soul that contradicts the Word of God. I surrender my beliefs and I choose truth."

Though your blueprint might be built on culture's toxic generalizations., God wants you to pull them down, cast them out, and rebuild with truth.

> *"By actively challenging the wrong meanings we've attached to life's experiences, we begin renewing the mind..."*
>
> Dr. James D. Treadwell jr.

Here's an Example:

- Culture Generalization: "All men are dogs."

The Challenge: "There are men who fear God, love their families, and keep their word. Lord, help me see and value those men."

- Culture Generalization: "All women just want your money."

The Challenge: "There are women who are virtuous, walk in integrity, dignity, and purpose (Proverbs 31). Lord, help me honor and recognize them."

Let's break this down:

- Challenge the lying argument by questioning it's validity.
- Ask yourself, Is this true in all experiences? For instance, if you can find two or more examples where the generalization does not fit the definition of "Always"; you have stripped that generalization of it's power.
- Find a specific relationship truth in the scriptures and replace the generalization.

—We see this played out in Emma's life—

"Emma" grew up in a household filled with strong, outspoken women — her mother and three aunts. All single. All disappointed.

All determined to protect her from what they called "man-made heartbreak."

They told her, "Don't ever trust a man." "They all lie."

"You don't need a man unless you want heartbreak."

These weren't suggestions — they were survival strategies. Lessons Emma learned with auto recall, like multiplication table's. They shaped her expectations, walled off her heart, and made her fiercely independent... and emotionally unavailable.

By the time Emma hit her early 30s, she was educated, successful — and secretly lonely. Deep down, she wanted love. God-honoring love. But every time she got close, her inner alarms rang: *"You can't trust him. You're better off alone."*

That's when she sought help. In one session, she was asked to write down the strongest belief she had about men. She wrote:

"Men can't be trusted."

The coach challenged by asking; "Is that true in *all* cases, Emma? Can you think of two or more examples where that belief doesn't hold up?"

Emma paused to think. Then she replied, my pastor is Trustworthy. My best friend's husband- he is faithful and kind. My uncle is a steady, godly man who keeps his word. ***That moment was her turning point because those lies had been exposed.***

The generalizations had lost their power. From there, Emma began to challenge every lie and replace them with biblical truth. She became agressive and proactive in her fight to be governed by the word of God in her future relationship.

> *"She became agressive and proactive in her fight to be governed by the word of God"*

For instance, Each time a fear-based thought arose, she asked herself: "Is this thought biblical? Or is this pain pretending to be truth?"

With consistent prayer, coaching, journaling, and scriptural meditation, Emma's inner script changed. She became emotionally available — and healthy in hear relationship mindsets. She no longer judged a man by her mother's wounds, but by God's Word.

Now? She's engaged to a man who loves God, loves her and honors her boundaries. He leads in faith, and welcomes premarital counseling. Together, they're building their relationship on truth, not trauma. She often says, "I had to challenge the lie to change my life. And now I'm living in the love I once believed didn't exist."

Like Emma, you must challenge, debunk, and replace the culture's blueprint lies and arguments with the biblical blueprint.

Pray This

"Father God, I give You my relationship blueprint. Show me what to keep and what to tear down. I renounce every lie, argument, as well as every vow that didn't come from You. Rebuild me with Your truth. I thank you for helping me build my future relationship on the Rock so that when storms come, my relationship will stand. In Jesus' name, amen."

Journal This

- **Who taught you, through word or deed, what relationships should look like?**

- **What unhealthy vows have you made?**

- **What arguments are you now aware of that could be contrary to the word of God?**

- **What do you want God to rebuild and transform in your mindset?**

— JOURNAL YOUR RESPONSE BELOW —

-
-
-
-

Chapter 2
BIG TAKEAWAY

"I can't build a Godly relationship using Culture's Blueprint. <u>I must actively and agressively reject the arguments</u> that left unchecked will sabotage my relationships"

Transformational Affirmation Decrees to Renew Your Relationship Blueprint

Family, hear me: your words are tools. Every time you speak truth, you're laying a brick in the foundation of your future. Don't let culture keep building for you — take the hammer back. Speak life. Speak identity. Speak God's truth over your old blueprint and watch the shift begin. Let's build!

1. I am renewing my mind daily and building my relationship life on God's truth.

2. I release every toxic belief I inherited and embrace God's design for love and unity.

3. I break inner vows that no longer serve my healing or purpose.

4. I trust God to rebuild my mindset and guide me toward healthy relationship patterns.

5. I choose to see men and women through the lens of God's love and truth.

6. I attract relationships that align with God's will and protect my purpose.

7. I speak life over my future, knowing God's blueprint leads to lasting joy and peace.

8. I am free from my past — I am free to build a beautiful, happy, and healthy marriage.

9. I honor my season of renewal by walking in wisdom, patience, and discernment.

10. I am a wise builder, laying every brick of my future on the solid rock of God's Word.

Family, this is the work that changes everything. As you get your foundation right, you can build a healthy relationship, marriage, and family upon it. That's why you're here. And that's why I'm here with you.

-Coach Will

Now that you have started rebuilding your relationship blueprint — what happens when that blueprint clashes with everything the world around you believes about love, dating, and identity?

Chapter 3 is where it gets real.
We're pulling back the curtain on culture's loudest messages and exposing why they keep leading people into disappointment, dysfunction, and divorce. You'll discover the solid strength of the Kingdom of God way — and why it still works, even when it's not trending. — Let's Go.

Chapter 3

The Culture versus The Kingdom

"Relationship success will only come by exchanging worldly relationship values and mindsets for Kingdom values and mindsets"

Let's be honest: the dating world out there is wild. Though I am in my 30th year of happy, healthy marriage, I pay very close attention to the single lifestyle habits of this generation. I study my clients, psychological journals, media, and society's family and relationship trends. As it's often said, "It's rough out in them dating streets." It's predominantly due to culture's thrust to push its agenda and sweep the masses into what is culturally accepted regarding family rather than what is God ordained. As we learned in Chapter 2, culture's relationship-building blocks are lies that are doomed to fail anyone who builds on them. If you haven't noticed, culture tells you:

- Follow your feelings.
- Keep your options open.
- Look perfect.

- Hook up fast, move on faster.

And then somehow you're supposed to magically build a marriage that lasts? Seriously?...

Listen, if you've ever felt that tension and confusion, you are not crazy. It's real.

> *"if you follow the culture's pattern, you are guaranteed to get the culture's results — brokeness and dysfunction."*.

I remember a season in my own life when I tried to fit in with the culture. I was trying to date "the way all of my peers did" with no clear standards, no boundaries, no biblical focus — just "the vibes." What did that lead to? ... Confusion, heartbreak, and tons of regrets. I thought I was winning because I was getting attention and "Big Man on Campus" treatment. But really, I was losing. I was steadily giving away pieces of myself — emotionally, mentally, spiritually, and physically — without any real commitment or purpose.

"I learned the hard way"

I had to learn the hard way:

Family, hear me, if you follow the culture's pattern, you are guaranteed to get the culture's results. And culture's results are brokenness and dysfunction.

You may relate. Maybe you've been told to "Protect yourself and never trust anyone fully." "You're only valuable if you look a certain way." **Here's a Big One.** "Sex is just sex — no big deal, everyone does it." "It's better to have someone than to be alone." Culture lures you to accept its patterns while causing you to *ignore red flags, and the lack of values and standards in the one it wants you to end up settling for.*

Those are culture's lies, dressed up to look like wisdom. It's just "tasty bait." But it'll leave you emptier and more confused than ever.

The Kingdom of God is different.

It calls you to a higher standard — not because God is angry and wants to spoil your fun, but because He is the best Father ever and wants to protect your heart.

The father calls us to a different pattern. It is a call to pursue honor over hype. The call to value covenant over convenience. To build relationships on trust and Godly purpose —not just feelings

Romans 12:2 says:

"Do not conform to the pattern of this world, but be transformed by the renewing of your mind." That means you can be single, you can date, and you can do it with purpose, with a goal — on God's terms, not the world's.

Kingdom versus Culture

Family, let's get real about what we're building on. In the Kingdom of God, everything we build, including relationships, is meant to be built on the Word of God. The "Word"is the Rock. It's unshakeable, unfailing, and eternal. When the winds blow, and you'd better believe they will blow, your relationship will stand because it was built on God's word and principles. But culture? Culture pushes something totally different. It tells you to build on vibes, energy, fun, appearance, and chemistry. That's why you'll hear:

- "If the vibe is off, then *dip*." (meaning leave")
- "If the vibe and energy feel good, this must be 'the one."
- "If the energy isn't right, it's a red flag."
- "If they are 'hot', 'look good', or 'fine'- jump in!"
- "If it's not fun, you should *bounce*." (meaning "leave")

- "If you're having fun and have things in common, you have hit the relationship jackpot!"

That sounds nice, but it's like building on sand.

So, let me break this down for you:
- Vibe is just a grain of sand
- Energy is a grain of sand
- Fun is a grain of sand
- Good Looks are grains of sand
- Having Things in common are grains of sand

Understand that sand shifts. Sand washes away. Sand is extremely unstable. Family, when you construct with cultural building materials and storms hit your relationship, ie., stress, loss, sickness, financial struggle — that relationship house built on sand will collapse every time. Having those things are ok as the decoration or the cherry on top of the relationship you want to build, but never as the foundation. Building on them is like building on sand.

"The Undertow Principle"

Allow me to teach you something, I call the Undertow Principle: When you stand on sand — even on a calm day — the smallest wave can break the sand apart that is under your feet. You can feel it shifting. Though many enjoy the sensation of the sand breaking apart under their feet, the truth is that it should serve as a warning. The warning of potential devastation. If you ignore that warning, the undertow — a hidden, powerful current beneath the surface can pull you out to sea. It can pull you out into the sea of culture, with all its confusion, heartbreak, and compromise.

Most people feel that subtle shifting under their feet but ignore it, just like they ignore red flags when a relationship is built on vibe, energy, and other shifting grains of sand instead of the firm foundation of God's Word. Family, don't ignore the undertow. It can sweep you further away from your values and your purpose than you ever imagined. God wants you to build on the Rock — His Word — so you don't get blown away when things get tough.

"The Word of God is The Rock It's Unshakable It's Unfailing It's Stable It's Eternal"

This is a demonstration of His love for you.

Jesus said:

"Everyone who hears these words of mine and puts them into practice is like a wise builder who built their establishment on the rock but those who hear and choose to build culture's way is a foolish builder who build their establishment on sand."

(Matthew 7:24-25)

Jesus describes the difference between wise and foolish builders. He places emphasis on the ability to hear and do what He says. I can say from personal experience that it takes an open and willing heart to not only gain head knowledge but to put what you are taught into practice through obedience.

Listen family, this is where the rubber meets the road. The place where you make an intentional decision for the sake of your upcoming relationship, marriage and family's destiny. It requires a conscious decision to choose the Kingdom of God building strategy over the building tactics of this world's culure that will crumble during life's changes, challenges and transitions. "So — Be Wise."

Count the cost of your decision.

Family, the choices we make are expensive. Very Expensive. If you choose to allow yourself to be swept up in the culture's undertow and rip current, there is a definate emotional, mental, physical and spiritual, and generational price to pay. However, the cost for building your relationships according to the Kingdom of God's principles is simple. It cost "mind renewal."

Jesus said, "which of you, wanting to build a tower, doesn't first sit down and count the cost of whether you have enough to complete it? Otherwise, when you have laid a foundation and you are not able to finish, all who see what you were building begin to mock you, saying, you tried to build this tower but could not finish.

I believe, this is a depiction of the state of the marriage union. The marriage covenant that is ordained of God has become polluted by culture's inferior building materials and the subsequent mockery due to the inability to finish the marriage and family course that was started. We have to do better. Note that the mockery is in direct relationship to not counting the cost resulting in not finishing. This looks alot like the 50% of first marriages ending in divorce, married households dropped from 71% down to 47% over a 50 year span according to the U.S. Census. Abuse, neglect, and family breakdown rates are out of control.

> "marriage has been polluted by culture's inferior building materials"

So you may ask how do I count the cost when building a relationship? Remember what you have learned in chapter 1. You exchanged your mindset of viewing being single as lonliness and punishment to believing that it is your season of preparation. And in chapter 2, you began the process of renewing your relationship blueprint. A major cost to count is settling the issue of "Just how willing you are to do relationship God's way?" That is counting the cost. As you allow this book and it's exercises to encourage and empower you to renew your mind, you are counting the cost and gathering what it takes to "finish.".

Now that we've exposed how culture's building materials are inferior and sure to fail and laid the foundation for how to build relationship the Kingdom of God way, I commend you for progressing to this point. As you are learning, I am learning about you. I know you're not trying to keep doing what doesn't work. You're not trying to play around with your heart, your time, or your calling. You're not here to copy culture — you're here to build something Kingdom. So now,. the question becomes: How should I date being that I am serious about doing it God's way?

Well, I'm glad you asked...

Let me give you the dating framework I personally lived by — and currently use when I coach singles who are serious about breaking cycles and building relationships God's way.

The Kingdom "D.A.T.E." Framework

— Discover with Discernment

— Assess with Accountability

— Test for Truth

— Engage with Intentionality to Establish with Wisdom

*This following Table gives an overview of the approach you should take when considering someone as a possible relationship partner.

The Kingdom D.A.T.E. Framework

| **D** | Discover | with Discernment |

Be informed spiritually and mentally to clarify who someone is before becoming emotionally invested.

| **A** | Assess | with Accountability |

To Reveal patterns and promote wise evaluation through community and spiritual counsel.

| **T** | Test | for Truth |

Uncover authentic character through real-life pressure, instead of surface-level charm.

| **E** | Engage | to Establish Wisdom |

Encourages clarity and purpose, ensuring your time and heart are invested in alignment with God's will.

D.A.T.E.
— A Kingdom Framework for Relationship Readiness —

This isn't casual dating. This isn't chasing vibes. This is dating with spiritual clarity, emotional intelligence, and God-honoring purpose. Here's how it goes:

D – Discover with Discernment

Before you catch feelings, seek clarity. Discover who someone is — not just who they post to be. Discern what spirit they carry. Ask: Is this someone who pushes me toward God or pulls me away? Learn their character, not just their conversation.
"The discerning heart seeks knowledge…" – Proverbs 15:14
Practice This: Pray before you pursue. Ask the Holy Spirit to show you what's beneath the surface.

A – Assess with Accountability

Don't try to assess someone's readiness for covenant while you're caught up in emotional fog. Invite godly counsel. Ask trusted voices to help you evaluate what you're seeing. Patterns tell the truth — not promises. Assess alignment in values, habits, and vision. Don't do this alone.
"Plans fail for lack of counsel, but with many advisers they succeed." – Proverbs 15:22
Practice This: Schedule regular check-ins with mentors or spiritual leaders as you date.

T – Test for Truth

Pressure reveals what pleasure hides. You can't really know someone until you see them under pressure, in conflict, and when the answer is "no." Test for integrity, not just interest. Watch how they handle your boundaries, feedback, and truth.
"You will know them by their fruit." – Matthew 7:16

Practice This: Allow time and situations to test their fruit — not just how they make you feel.

E – Engage with Intentionality to Establish with Wisdom

Don't date for fun. Date with a God-centered purpose. When you engage, do it with clarity. Communicate goals. Set healthy boundaries. Invite the Holy Spirit into the process. You're not here to play — you're here to establish a firm foundation with wisdom. This is preparation, not performance.

"By wisdom a house is built, and through understanding it is established." – Proverbs 24:3

Practice This: Ask, "What are we building?" If there's no vision, there's no direction.

Remember, you're not dating just to pass time and if you are considering dating, you must commit to dating the Kingdom of God's way. Don't hand your future over to vibes and emotion. Use discernment. Cooperate with accountability. Test for truth and observe the fruit. Engage with purpose. This is what it looks like to date as a Kingdom builder. This is how you stop repeating patterns… and start preparing for promise.

Family,
by cooperating with this process, you are on the right path to being an example of relationship and marriage by God's building design.
Now it's time to get active!

Do This

- **Write down three cultural messages you've believed about relationships.**

1. _____
2. _____
3. _____

- **Ask: "Do thes messages align with God's Word or do they "Argue against it?"**

- _____
  _____
  _____

- **Choose Kingdom principle to replace it.**

- _____
  _____
  _____

Commit to practicing that principle the next time you interact with someone you're interested in.

For example:

Culture says: "If they're hot, or if they're fine -go for it."
Kingdom says: "If they're godly, consider them, with accountability."

PrayThis

"Lord, help me see through and detect culture's arguements and lies. Give me the courage to consider a relationship with purpose, to guard my heart, and to trust You with my future. I trade confusion for clarity. I choose Your Kingdom pattern over the world's pattern. In Jesus' name, amen."

Journal This

Reflection Considerations

Before you move on, take a moment to slow down and lean in. These reflection questions aren't just "homework" — they're heart work. They are designed to help you dig beneath the surface, confront what's been shaping your thoughts, and invite God into your process of mind renewal. Let's go!

- **How has culture shaped my relationship patterns?**

- **As I am progressing, what do I need to leave behind?**

- **What does God say about how I should build relationships? Do I agree with HIM?**

—JOURNAL YOUR RESPONSE BELOW—

-
-
-
-

Chapter 3

BIG TAKEAWAY

> "Everything in God's Kingdom is to be built upon God's Word"
>
> ---
>
> "The Undertow of culture can pull you further away from God's plan for your relationship then you can imagine"
>
> ---
>
> "I will end my conformity to the world's approach to relationships by allowing my Mind to be Renewed by the Word of God."

Transformational Affirmation Decrees for Kingdom of God Relationship Mindsets

Let's be real — This Culture is loud. But the Kingdom is louder when you give it voice. You can't fight culture's pull with silence. You need to decree your allegiance out loud. Speak these decrees daily. Think of them as Kingdom bricks — every declaration is another step out of culture's undertow and into God's divine design for your relationship life. Ready?
Let's go.

1. I reject culture's lies and boldly embrace Kingdom truth in my relationships.
2. I build on God's Word, instead of vibes, energy, or shifting emotions.
3. I recognize red flags and refuse to ignore them or make excuses.
4. I am a wise builder who follows God's blueprint for love, connection, and purpose.
5. I value covenant over convenience and purpose over popularity.
6. I resist being swept away by culture's undertow — I stand firm on the Rock of God's truth.
7. I choose honor, trust, and intentionality in every connection I make.
8. I guard my heart and steward my emotions with wisdom and discernment.
9. I let go of false cultural patterns and embrace God's standard for lasting love.
10. I am being transformed daily by the renewing of my mind, and I walk in Kingdom confidence.

Family,
Culture may appear to have a pull on this generation, but your relationship purposes are bigger, stronger, and more powerful than the hype. That is because God Almighty is for your relationship success. You are called to build a relationship and marriage that lasts, that is stable, and endures.
That happens when you build God's way and I'm here to help you do it.

By now, you've started seeing through culture's games — the hype, the emotional fluff, the shaky foundations. You're choosing Kingdom over chaos.
That's huge.

But here's the next question: Who are you becoming while you wait for "the one"? Because before you build anything strong with someone else, God wants to build something whole in you. What if you've been waiting on a relationship to complete you…
when God's been waiting for you to heal with Him?

In chapter 4, we are drilling deeper than dating habits. We're going straight into identity — that root place where confidence, healing, and self-worth are born.
— Let's Go

Chapter 4

—IDENTITY—
Wholeness Before Oneness

*"God's will is that you be whole
before you become One"*

---

*I*f you've ever thought, *"I'll finally feel whole once I meet the right person,"* you're not alone. Almost all of us have bought that lie at some point. It's everywhere — movies, songs, even family comments like *"You just need to find your other half."* But can I tell you the truth?

God never intended for you to live as a <u>half-person</u>, waiting for someone else to complete you.

I can remember a time when I thought getting married would solve all my problems. I figured if I had a wife, I'd feel valuable, strong, respected — like a "real man." But deep down, I was still wrestling with insecurity, fear, and past wounds. I didn't know it yet, but no spouse — no matter how amazing — could heal those places in me. God had to teach me:

"Son, you are already whole in Me. Marriage doesn't fix your issues — it reveals them."

That was a wake-up call. With the help of my mentor, I was able to face my baggage, be honest, and do the healing work. I had to learn to love who I was in Christ before I tried to build a future with someone else.

Maybe for you, the lies sound like this:

- *"If I had a good man, I'd feel loved and secure."*
- *"If I had a good woman, I'd finally feel valued."*
- *"If I were married, my family would respect me."*

Those are deep longings — and they're human. But they can become traps if you think another person is your fix.

This may sting a bit. But, it is this worldly culture that pushes the "you complete me" fantasy. But God says, *"You are complete in Me."*

Mind Renewal Opportunity
Colossians 2:10 says:

"You are complete in Him,
who is the head of all principality and power."

That means that as a single person doing the renewal work and surrendered to God's will and way **You are already complete**. Understand this. It is Jesus Christ who makes us whole. No human can define your worth. No relationship can replace your identity in Christ. When you walk in that truth, you show up healthy. You show up secure. You show up confident. You are not waiting to be rescued — you're already standing strong.

> **"You are not half of a person waiting for another half. You are complete in Him."**

"Kingdom Math"

Wholeness Before Oneness

Family, lean in to this — because this right here will change the way you look at relationships. God says, *"the two shall become one."* That is Kingdom math. In God's Kingdom, $1 + 1 = 1$.

Let me break that down. One whole, healed, "Christ-secured" person joined to another whole, healed, "Christ-secured" person equals one strong, unified, and healthy marriage relationship. **That's Kingdom math.**

But the world pushes a broken equation:

- *"I'm half of a person."*
- *"They'll complete me."*
- *"Two halves make a whole."*

"These are Lies"

> **"Two half-healed people don't make a whole —
> they make dysfunction"**

If you come into a relationship as a 0.5, or a 0.25, hoping someone else will patch your brokenness, you'll keep pulling from each other's emptiness and wonder why things feel chaotic. **God's design is wholeness before oneness.** That means you are complete in Christ first, standing whole, before you unite with another whole person. That's how Kingdom relationships thrive — and how they last.

The Fix-It Syndrome

Family, allow me to share something else I've seen over and over again. I call it the **"Fix-It Syndrome."** Maybe you've heard it said like this:

- *"If I just love them enough, they'll change."*
- *"They have so much potential — I can fix them."*
- *"Once we get together, they'll straighten up."*

Listen, family: that is a **trap.**

The Fix-It Syndrome shows up when you ignore the fact that the person you're interested in is not whole, not healed, *and* not willing to do the healing work.

The Fix-It Syndrome will have you trying to be their therapist, their rescuer, their pastor, their motivator — instead of their partner. And that is not how God designed relationships.

Think of it like a plumber working on a leaky faucet. While he's trying to patch that one leak, the entire pipe bursts — and suddenly, he is drowning in problems that were never his responsibility to begin with. That's what happens when you try to *fix* someone who doesn't even want to be fixed — you get overwhelmed, exhausted, and eventually hurt. There is a **big difference** between someone who is still learning, but has a *willing* and *open* heart to grow in God's ways — and someone who is resistant, closed off, and deeply tied to culture's patterns.

Family, hear me:

- It is **NOT** your job to rescue someone from what they refuse to leave.
- It is **NOT** your job to try to transform someone who is not willing to surrender to God's mind renewal process.

God calls us to partner with people who are willing to renew their minds, who want to heal, who are teachable and open. The Fix-It Syndrome will keep you stuck trying to repair what only God can transform — and what only a willing heart will allow. If you sense you are falling into that Fix-It pattern, pause. Take it to prayer. And remember — you were called to *love*, not to *rescue*.

Brett & The Fix-It Syndrome

Brett was a good man — dependable, spiritually grounded, and full of potential. He had been through his own healing journey after a toxic relationship in college, and when he met Missy, he was convinced that this time would be different. Missy was stunning, charismatic, and passionate. But she was also volatile, deeply insecure, and rooted in past trauma she had no intention of facing. Brett noticed the red flags early: emotional outbursts, subtle manipulation, unwillingness to take responsibility, and a tendency to blame everyone else — including him for her past pain and present behaviors. But Brett didn't walk away. **Why? Because he believed his love could fix her.** He stepped into the relationship as her counselor, her spiritual guide, her motivator. He prayed for her. He encouraged her. He even bought her books on healing and set up sessions for her to talk to someone. But Missy never showed up for those appointments — she said she didn't need them.

Brett kept investing, even as his peace began to drain. He was exhausted, confused, and spiritually dry. **What started as compassion became codependency.** And when the relationship finally crumbled, Brett didn't just walk away heartbroken — he walked away disillusioned. He now questions if healthy love even exists. Not because love failed him — but because he stepped into a role God never asked him to play.

Brett tried to fix what only surrender and mind renewal could repair. And he learned, painfully, that loving someone doesn't mean saving them.

His journey isn't over. But now he's learning that true partnership begins with two people already submitted to God's healing process — not one trying to drag the other there.

Isaiah & Francine
Seeking Wholeness Before the "Yes"

Isaiah and Francine met in the most unexpected place — at a relationship workshop hosted by a local church. Both had come with baggage. Isaiah had grown up watching his father manipulate women and treat relationships like trophies. He learned how to perform but never how to be emotionally present. Francine had survived emotional abuse and betrayal in her last relationship. She had trust issues and unresolved self-worth struggles. But here's what made them different: they didn't run from their issues.
They faced them — head-on.

Before they even exchanged numbers, they both agreed: "I'm still healing." Instead of jumping into something romantic, they spent time in separate coaching programs, receiving wise counsel, unpacking cultural lies, and confronting blind spots with accountability. They journaled, served in their church, and dug deep into who they were becoming — not just who they wanted to be with.

Months later, when they reconnected, something had shifted. They weren't trying to fill each other's gaps — they were overflowing with the fruit of growth. Conversations were honest. Boundaries were respected. Their connection wasn't trauma-driven — it was purpose-led.

Today, Isaiah and Francine are married. Not perfect — but thriving. They still meet monthly with their marriage mentors. They still practice healthy communication. And they still testify that the time they took for healing before oneness was the best investment they could've made. They say, "We weren't rescuing each other we were preparing for each other."

These two stories paint a powerful contrast: one chose to rescue, the other chose to be restored.

> *"Wholeness before oneness isn't just a nice idea — it's the difference between cycles of pain and a foundation that lasts"*

So where do you see yourself?

Maybe you're like Brett:

You love hard. You believe in people. You want to see them healed and whole. But somewhere along the way, you've become the fixer — trying to pull someone along who isn't ready or willing to grow. Here's what you need to do:

— Take a step back and surrender the need to be someone's savior.

— Seek godly counsel and ask, "Am I helping... or enabling?"

— Give the person to God in prayer and allow Him to work — without trying to do His job.

— Reinvest in your own wholeness, identity, and boundaries. You are not called to be "consumed" by someone else's healing journey.

Maybe you're more like Missy

You recognize that someone has tried to fix you. Maybe they've exhausted themselves trying to help — but deep down, you haven't fully surrendered to the healing process.

Here's your invitation:

— Humble yourself, acknowledge the resistance and ask yourself, "What am I afraid of facing and healing?"

— Release the idea that someone else can do the work for you.

— Begin to take responsibility for your growth — spiritually, emotionally, and mentally.

— Pray and ask God to soften your heart as you take the responsibility of renewing your mind. Let the Word of God through community, and accountability lead your transformation.

Or maybe, just maybe... you're like Isaiah and Francine

You're doing the work. You've realized that healing takes time, and you're walking it out with accountability, wisdom, and intention.

Here's your encouragement:

— Keep going. Don't rush the process just because you feel ready.

— Stay under mentorship. Let godly counsel continue to shape your path. Remember, this is a forever process

— Ask God to align your next steps with His timing — not your timeline.

— Stay focused on becoming before bonding. You are testimony of "Kingdom Math" where (1 + 1 = 1)

Pray This:

"Father God, thank You that I am already complete in You. I renounce every lie that says I am half of a person and need to be completed by someone. Teach me to live from a place of wholeness. Help me grow into the person You've called me to be, so I can build healthy, purposeful relationships in Your timing.

Journal This

- Where do I look for my sense of worth? What scripture supports this?

- What truth does God speak over me? What argument do I hear against that truth?

- Have I ever felt responsible for someone else's healing? What did it cost me emotionally or spiritually?

- Am I truly open to mind renewal, or am I waiting for someone else to do the work for me? What's stopping me from taking full responsibility for my growth?

—JOURNAL YOUR RESPONSE BELOW—

-
-
-
-

In Jesus' name, amen."

Chapter 4
Big takeaway

> *"God wants me whole before I am one. My identity is secure in Christ I am Complete in Him."*

Transformational Affirmation Decrees

for

Healing Your Heart — Before You Join Hearts

Family, healing isn't passive — it's *intentional*. You can't wait for your heart to heal itself. You have to *partner with God* in the process. And one of the most powerful ways to do that is by speaking the truth out loud. These decrees help you replace trauma's lies with God's truth. Say them daily. Let them reshape your inner blueprint and prepare you to love from a place of wholeness and strength- not survival.

1. I am healing deeply and completely through God's love and truth.

2. I resist being led by trauma or pain — I embrace being led by God's purpose and peace.

3. I choose relationships that reflect God's purposes for my life.

4. I am free from emotional bondage and being drawn to dysfunction.

5. I attract healthy love because I value myself the way God values me.

6. I set wise boundaries that protect my heart and preserve my peace.

7. I release old soul ties and replace them with Kingdom alignment.

8. I recognize and reject trauma bonds disguised as love.

9. I trust God to guard my heart and lead me into healthy covenant connection.

10. I love from a whole place, not a hurting one

— and my future is secure in Him.

Family, the most powerful relationship you will ever have is the one you have with God, and with yourself through Him. When you build that foundation, you'll never have to settle again.

You've just done some serious inner work. You've looked in the mirror. Faced the truth. And maybe, for the first time, started seeing yourself as whole — not waiting to be completed, but choosing healing, identity, and transformation.

But now comes the next challenge…Who will you align with — and why? Because the moment you begin to walk in wholeness, your preferences will get loud:

"She's my type."
"He checks all my boxes."
"This just feels right."

But here's the truth:

"Not everything that looks right is assigned to your purpose."

Chapter 5

Purpose Over Preference

"Your preferences and type must align with God's preordained will for your life."

Have you ever wondered why you keep being drawn to the same kind of person, even when it never works out? You might call it your "type." But can I challenge you for a minute? **What if your "type" is just a reflection of your wounds?**
There was a season when I kept attracting the same patterns — people who made me feel needed, admired, and in control. It felt good at first, but in the end, those relationships left me empty.

Why? Because my "type" was rooted in my own brokenness. I was drawn to people who had the same fears and dysfunctions I hadn't healed from — and we trauma-bonded around them.

We called it "chemistry," but it was really just *common wounds*. We thought we had so much in common, but what we had in common was pain and past disappointments.

Family, I need you to catch this:
Far too many of you keep choosing people who look like your trauma. They feel familiar. They make you feel seen in your broken places — because they have the *same* broken places. That is not the Kingdom of God pattern. That is a "trauma bond."

> **"too many of you keep choosing people who look like your trauma"**

God doesn't want you to build your future with someone who will help and assist you in remaining resentful, bitter, or stuck. He wants you to build with someone who will help you heal, even if that person is very different from what you consider your usual "type."

"They Just Get Me..."

Family, let's dig even deeper into the presentation of trauma bonds. One of the most deceptive voices of a trauma bond is the little phrase: *"They just get me."* You might feel drawn to someone and say, *"I want to be with them because they get me."* — and that feels so comforting.

But here's what I've seen in my life and in my work as a therapist and coach:

> **"Sometimes the reason they "get" you is because they carry the exact same unhealed trauma wound that you do."**

Now, don't get me wrong — having a similar trauma history is not automatically a red flag. The *real* question is:

- *Has this person walked through healing?*
- *Have they renewed their mind, or are they still stuck in trauma.*

If they're still bleeding from the same place, the "understanding and pampering" of your wounds can pull you both back into a cycle of dysfunction. This is a type of *False Empathy* — or trauma in with an empathetic disguise. Remember, trauma and past wounds don't just live in your memories; they carry energy, a frequency, and a vibration. It can be sensed, felt, and if allowed will lead you with clouded vision. Culture pushes and lures you into matching energies by enticing you to look for someone with your same vibe, the same spark. But sometimes that "vibe" is trauma in disguise.

In my experience as a therapist, I've done extensive study of family patterns. This includes children in foster care whose parents were also in foster care. They were often drawn to partners with matching trauma and pain because it felt familiar. For clarity, when I say "matching trauma", it doesn't mean their traumas were identical or from the same scenarios. Rather, it means that their traumas subconsciously united perfectly to play out the same dysfunctional family dynamics that both parties were raised within. That offers a familiarity that can seem safe. Still, it can be dangerous if there is no pursuit of healing, no community to help you transform, no accountability to break free from the old patterns.

> **"Unhealed pain recognizes and is drawn to unhealed pain."**

"Unhealed pain recognizes and is magnetically drawn to unhealed pain."

God wants you to be a whole, healed person before you join yourself to someone else — not bond together from a place of brokenness.

How Trauma Bonds Can Hold You Captive

Many people pursue, get tripped up, and remain entangled in toxic relationships not because they *want* to stay, but because something deeper has taken root. According to Dutton and Painter (1993), "The power imbalance is created and sustained from the victim's dependency and powerlessness to the perpetrator who has absolute control and dominance over the victim; fueled by the perpetrator's intermittent good-bad treatment cycle of abuse, in which trauma bonding dysfunction is at its most powerful and interferes with the victim wanting to leave and influences the victim to stay."

Let's unpack that.

When someone treats you sweet one minute and disrespectful the next—*and you stay*—you might be caught in a trauma bond. Why? Because the kindness gives you hope, while the abuse keeps you hooked. That cycle of confusion creates *dependency*. Now let me put it in plain terms:

"Trauma bonding happens when someone gains control over your heart by creating a cycle of confusion – being kind one minute and cruel the next. That drama fueled back-and-forth dance breaks you down over time. It zaps your strength and the more powerless you feel, the harder it becomes to walk away. This isn't love. It's manipulation – and it thrives and is enabled when you're depending on a person instead of depending on God."

When we don't understand real love—**God's love**—we start mistaking toxic behavior for passion, drama for excitement, and inconsistency expression for chemistry. But true love doesn't keep you guessing. It builds you up, instead of breaking you down.

Ro'Shea's Story: "When Healing Changes the Taste"

Ro'Shea used to say she liked her men "with edge." She didn't feel safe unless he had a little danger in him — the kind of man who wouldn't back down from a fight, could handle himself in the streets, and wore his trauma like a badge of honor. To her, drama felt like passion. Explosive arguments meant love and attention. Chaos meant commitment.

They used to say, "We fight hard, but we love harder." But all Ro'Shea ever walked away with were bruised feelings, broken promises, and deeper soul wounds. It wasn't until she entered counseling that she realized: She was mistaking intensity for intimacy. She was feeding on adrenaline, not actual love, and was bonding through mutual dysfunction — not shared purpose.

Her healing journey was tough becaue she had to end the relationship, and turn her focus to confronting the trauma she saw growing up. Then and only then did she realize that the yelling, the controlling, the chaos felt like home. To Ro'shea, that was leaving what was familiar and secure. But over time, something amazing happened:

What she found attractive started to change. Suddenly, stability didn't feel boring — it felt safe. Consistency didn't feel weak — it felt strong. A man who prayed and offered solutions from the bible caused her to feel cared for. She is confidently enjoying her single season, knowing that she is investing in her future marriage by healing and allowing her preference to be shaped by God's purpose.

Ro'Shea's story is powerful because it reminds us that when you're healed, your "type" starts to align with your purpose. And that's not just psychology — that's Bible. That's God's design.

Let's look at Jesus.

Think about Jesus and the disciples. He didn't choose people who looked the same, acted the same, or thought the same. He chose people who would challenge, refine, could *build* together, and agree together on the things that truly mattered. Jesus' type were those who believed in the his purpose, and could unite together with him to accomplish that purpose Jesus was sent to fulfill. The same is true with our relationships. Agreement focused on God's intent for relationship and marriage is paramount. Dr. Bill Hamon says,

> *"God created us to share the true Agape Love that can only be demonstrated by giving of oneself. The same goes for marriage Love. If you married to make yourself happy – you're probably on the edge of divorce. Because true marriage Love is like Agape Love that wants to bless your spouse, and give yourself for them."*

Before entering a relationship, agreement with God's pupose for the relationship must be achieved.

Please understand that all agreement is not made equal. What you agree on together is paramount. Amos 3:3 says: *"Can two walk together unless they are agreed?"*

Yes, you need agreement, but not agreement about common dysfunction. You don't need agreement to support your resentment and unforgiveness. You need agreement about God's purpose and mission for your lives. You need agreement about mind renewal and healing. You need someone who will be in agreement with you about honoring God with your relationship. Sometimes the person God sends will feel unfamiliar because they *do not* feed your wounds. They call you higher. They point you to your purpose. They don't coddle your bitterness; instead, they challenge it. That's love.

Do This:

1: Write down the description of your "type" — physically, emotionally, spiritually.

___

2: Ask yourself, *"Where did I learn to crave this?"*

___

3: List the ways these patterns have harmed you or slowed your growth.

___

4: Describe the kind of partner who would *heal*, challenge, and support your purpose — even if they don't look like your "type."

___

5: Pray and ask God to help you to see beyond the familiar.

Pray This:

"God, I surrender every unhealthy soul tie, every trauma bond, every preference rooted in my wounds. Break them. Heal me. Show me Your pattern for my relationships. Open my eyes to the partners You have assigned to my purpose, even if they do not match my old type. Give me courage to choose differently.

In Jesus' name, amen."

Journal This

- Have I confused shared trauma for true connection?

- What patterns have felt familiar but unhealthy?

- Am I willing to accept someone who might be different, but sent by God to help me heal?

- What are two things I can practice to stay focused on God's purpose while entertaining a possible relationship?

—JOURNAL YOUR RESPONSE BELOW—

Big takeaway

> "My purpose must lead my preferences. I will choose mind renewal, healing and wholeness over familiarity."

Transformational Affirmation Decrees to Align Your Preferences to God's Purposes

Family, your preferences and type must align with God's preordained will for your life. The day for allowing cultural trends and the gravitational pull of trauma bonds to dictate to your relationship desire is over. Affirm these transformational truths.

1. My preferences are being purified to align with God's plan for my life and legacy.
2. I am free from trauma bonds — I recognize aaadysfunction and no longer call it love.
3. I desire what is good, godly, and growth-producing in a relationship.
4. I release bitterness and make room for healing, growth, and joy.
5. I choose to heal, not to harbor pain.
6. I walk in love and mercy without letting past wounds direct my future.
7. I cancel the power of offense over my heart and mind.
8. I trust God to be my defender and restorer.
9. I am being refined by His purpose.
10. I am free — mentally, emotionally, physically, and spiritually — through the power of forgiveness.

Family, listen — trauma will always try to rewrite your preferences to match your pain. But you are called to more than surviving patterns. You are called to build something that honors God and heals your future

for generations to come..

―――――――――――――――――――――――――

So far, we've confronted culture, exposed toxic blueprints, and realigned our identity with God's truth. But now — it's time to deal with one of the most misunderstood and misrepresented concepts in today's world: "LOVE"

Is love a feeling? Is commitment still sacred? Does sacrifice mean losing yourself? And what exactly is covenant, anyway?

In Chapter 6, we're tearing down the false images of love that have kept so many bound in emotional confusion, failed relationships, and soul-level exhaustion.

We're going to discover that God's version of love isn't shallow — it's sacred.

It's not built on hype — but on honor.

Not on emotional highs — but on covenant and character.

If you've ever loved the wrong way... or wondered why love hasn't lasted for you in the past — this next chapter is your healing space.

CHAPTER 6

Redefining Love
Commitment, Sacrifice & Covenant

"It's Time to Learn Love – God's Way"

Let's be real.
Most of us grew up thinking love was about feeling something.
That spark. The butterflies. The excitement. But here's the truth nobody told us: Feelings fade. God stays. If "love" is built only on a spark, it will burn out. But if it's built on God and his word, it lasts.
I used to think passion meant love. If she made my heart race, I was all in. But what I didn't understand was that no matter how amazing someone seemed, if my love for God wasn't bigger than my love for them, I couldn't truly love them the right way. In my own marriage, the reason we've been able to stand for decades isn't because I'm so great or my wife is perfect — it's because we both love God more than we love each other.

Just let that sink in...

- I love God more than I love my wife.
- She loves God more than she loves me.

And because of that, we can love each other well. God is the linchpin. God is the glue. God is love itself. When I love Him first, I love my wife through His love — with grace, forgiveness, and patience I couldn't drum up on my own.

Culture says:

> *"It's not about having a perfect love story, but finding someone who matches your madness."*

But the Bible says:

"We love others because we experience that He first loved us."

(1 John 4:19)

If you don't have God's love living in you, you will run out of patience. You will run out of kindness. You will run out of grace. This is because human love with all of its effort is limited — but God's love is limitless.

If you want a relationship that can weather storms, you have to love God first. That love overflows into how you love yourself, and then how you love someone else.

Cultural Love vs. God's Love

Family, let's get real. Our culture has been deeply damaged by anthems, images, and depictions of false love. We really don't understand what true love actually is anymore because, in society, we have abandoned God's definition of love as found in 1 Corinthians chapter 13. Love has been downgraded to something superficial, reduced to a feeling, or written off as a "second-hand emotion." And with all due respect to the legendary Tina Turner, her song asking "What's love got to do with it?" drilled deep into a generation's psyche, convincing young and old minds alike that love was just a fleeting feeling or a weak emotion.

But I disagree — respectfully, I disagree.

"Love is not an emotion at all. Love is not a feeling. It is a command of Almighty God"

Jesus commanded us to love one another, and 1 Corinthians 13 tells us exactly what that looks like. True love is God's love, because God is love. Period. End of story.

For a world desperately searching to experience love, the truth is this: You will never experience true love until you tap into God Himself.

Love is not butterflies in the stomach. Love is not a twinkle in the eye. Love is not a sexual encounter. Love is the essence of who God is. It's not only what He does, but it who He is. And if we are going to reflect Him, then we must become love in action and "Be Love", just as He is the pure essence of love.

"Love is not only what God does—It's Who HE is"

Emotional Love vs. Covenant Love

Let's pause right here, family. Because this part is critical. We need to separate two very different kinds of love: Emotional love and Covenant love.

Emotional love says:
- "I love you because of how you make me feel."
- "I love you when you treat me well."

- "I love you... until I don't feel it anymore."

Emotional love feels real — but it's not reliable. It shifts with mood, with time, with frustration, with disappointment. It's based on circumstances and what's being received in the moment.And when feelings fluctuate (because they will), emotional love can and usually does disappear.

But Covenant love says something different:

- "I love you because God commands me to."
- "I love you as an act of commitment, not just chemistry."
- "I love you with patience, truth, and endurance — even when situations are tough."

Covenant love is God's kind of love. It's not just romantic or emotional — it's relational and sacrificial. Covenant love stays even when offended. Covenant love holds true even if emotions fluctuate. Even if you don't "feel in love" every single second of the day.

Emotional love feels - Covenant love chooses.

Covenant love doesn't come naturally — it's supernatural. And if we're going to walk in it, we must receive it from God first and live it out by renewing our minds.

> *Understand that relationships that thrive aren't built on the high of passion. They're built on the foundation of God's covenant, sealed with intentional choices every single day.*

Mind Renewal Opportunity

Let's revisit God's definition of love as described in 1 Corinthians 13:4-8. (Amplified)

4. "Love endures with patience and serenity, love is kind and thoughtful, and is not jealous or envious; love does not brag and is not proud or arrogant.

5. It is not rude; it is not self-seeking, it is not provoked [nor overly sensitive and easily angered]; it does not take into account a wrong endured.

6. It does not rejoice at injustice, but rejoices with the truth [when right and truth prevail].

7. Love bears all things [regardless of what comes], believes all things [looking for the best in each one], hopes all things [remaining steadfast during difficult times], endures all things [without weakening].

8. Love never fails [it never fades nor ends].

Family, there is something missing from this Kingdom of God description of LOVE.

Do you see what is missing? Here's a hint: It starts with an "F" and rhymes with "Ceilings". You got it! – *"FEELINGS"* are not an ingredient of this "Agape" Godly Love. In fact, putting aside your feelings and emotional responses is a sure way to operate in this Biblical Love. When Jesus is at the center, your relationship is built on a rock. When your partner loves God more than you, they will treat you better because they reverence and honor Him. When you love God more than your partner, you will forgive, serve, and sacrifice — because that's what God does for you.

Do This:

1: Ask yourself honestly, "Do I love God more than I love the idea of being loved by another person?"

_____
_____
_____

2: Meditate on what it would look, feel, and effect you to truly place God as the foundation of your relationship.*(Describe your experience below)*

_____
_____
_____
_____

3: Settle the issue that you will desire your future spouse would love God more than they love you. *(List any challenges you'd face)*

_____
_____
_____

4: Recommit to growing your intimacy with God, knowing that it is the source of all true love.

5: Practice God's love right now — don't wait for a relationship to start. I challenge you to intentionally practice the kind of love described in 1 Corinthians 13 toward your family, your friends, your coworkers, even strangers. If you can't live it daily, you can't carry it into a relationship. There's no better time than now to build your Love muscles.

Pray This

"Father God, thank You for loving me first. Teach me to love You above every person and every desire. Help me build relationships with you at the center. I commit to love others through Your heart, not just my feelings. I renew my mind so that I can be transformed into a person who can give covenant love because I am rooted in Your love.

In Jesus' name, amen."

Ponder This

- Do I truly love God first?
- How has loving Him helped me love others better?
- How does it feel to intentionally practice 1 Corinthians 13 love?
- Am I willing to build my relationship with God as the foundation for my future relationship?

Journal This

- Do I truly love God first?

- How has loving Him helped me love others better?

- How does it feel to intentionally practice 1 Corinthians 13 love?

- Am I willing to build my relationship with God as the foundation for my future relationship?

—JOURNAL YOUR RESPONSE BELOW—

Chapter 6
BIG TAKEAWAY

> *"Loving God first is the Only way to Truly Love Yourself & Anyone else Well."*

Transformational Affirmation Decrees
to Engrain God's Love as Your Source of Love

Take a deep breath and clear your heart of distractions. This moment is not about the counterfeit ideas the world has sold you — it's about embracing the truth of God's covenant design for love and marriage. These decrees will help you tear down cultural lies and rebuild your vision based on God's eternal Word. Say them slowly, believe them deeply, and let them transform how you see love, commitment, and your future.

1 Corinthians 13:4–8

1. I am patient and kind, because covenant love refuses to rush or wound.
2. I resist envy or boasting — God's Love Secures me.
3. I humble myself and resist pride, and self-centered thinking.
4. I resist being easily provoked, and allow kindness, and patience to rule my behavior.
5. I resist keeping score of wrongs; I choose forgiveness because love keeps no record of being wronged.
6. I look for the best, believe the best, and hope for the best for people
7. I let go of the need to be pursued by people who are not sent by God.
8. I cooperate with God's love in me that is patient, kind, and enduring.
9. The love I have for others reflects God's heart — It is strong, pure, and faithful.
10. I walk in covenant love that does not fade, and never fails.

> "Family, listen to me — if you get this one thing right, everything else will fall into place. Love God first, and you will have more than enough love to give your future spouse. That's the real foundation of a lasting healthy marriage."

Let's be real — in a culture that glorifies blurred lines, instant gratification, and "do what feels right," the words boundaries, purity, and honor sound old-school. But as my mentor, Dr. James D. Treadwell jr. says, "Old School Doesn't Mean Wrong School!" In fact, we are in a time of Reformation, where the truth of God that has been lost in cultural translation and mutation is being restored. We are on the front line bringing God's purposes back into the shape and form that HE intended.

Reformation of Godly relationship, marriage and family is on God's agenda and we are on the front line.

Understand that in the Kingdom — boundaries, purity, and honor are weapons of protection and pillars of purpose. In Chapter 7, we're going to flip the script on what the world says is outdated and rediscover God's sacred design for intimacy, discipline, and spiritual authority in relationships. This isn't just about rules — it's about recognizing your worth and setting a standard that aligns with your identity in Christ. If you've ever struggled to say no, felt ashamed about your past, or wondered how to guard your heart without becoming hard-hearted, this chapter is for you. Get ready to build a love that doesn't just feel good — but honors God.

Chapter 7

Boundaries, Purity, and Honor

*Protecting yourself and honoring God
with your relationship choices*

Let me be real with you — I wish someone had pulled me aside earlier in my life and told me the power of boundaries. Because the world will tell you boundaries are a buzzkill, that purity is old-fashioned and outdated, and that "exploring" yourself and others is normal. What they don't tell you is that a lack of boundaries can leave you broken, confused, and wounded in ways you never imagined.

But there's something even more dangerous than an obvious attack on purity — and that's a slow undertow of compromise. You can stand in the shallow water of culture, thinking you're safe, until one gentle wave begins to erode the ground beneath you. One compromise, one blurred line, one moment of silence when you should have spoken up. You don't feel the danger until you realize you've drifted far from God's design for love.

"Just like an undertow slowly pulls you out to sea, ignoring boundaries will slowly pull your heart away from God's best for your life."

There was a time when I believed as long as I was a "good person," I could make my own rules. If I thought I loved someone, then crossing lines wasn't a big deal, right?

But every time I stepped outside God's boundaries, I paid a price emotionally, spiritually, and mentally. And the worst part was, it made it harder to see my own worth — and harder to accurately see the other person's worth. God had to teach me the hard but beautiful truth: Boundaries aren't rejection — they are protection. Purity isn't about shame — it's about worship. And honor is about treating another person as someone God deeply values.

Family, I know how loud the culture is as it screams through media, society, and platforms:

- "Try it before you commit."
- "Sex is just sex…everybody is doing it."
- "Don't be so uptight."
- "Get with the times."

But what you must understand is that culture doesn't crash against you like a tidal wave. Rather, it slowly and subtly pulls on you. It's an undertow.

The moment you stop standing on the firm foundation of God's Word, your footing weakens. And if you ignore the shift under your feet, you'll be swept out into a sea of confusion, pain, and broken expectations. That's why the Word of God is your anchor, and why sexual sobriety must become your compass.

But God's standard is crystal clear in the Bible:

"For this is the will of God, your sanctification: that you abstain from sexual immorality…" (1 Thessalonians 4:3)

Sex is holy. It is designed for covenant, not casual. And boundaries? Boundaries don't trap you; they free you to love in a way that honors God and yourself.

Cultural Distortions and "Sex-pectations"

Let's talk real for a second. So many of us learned about sex and boundaries — or the lack of them — from the streets, from our peers, from the locker rooms, or from older siblings who themselves were misinformed. These were people who passed down broken scripts from generation to generation, leaving us confused, badly misinformed, and wounded.

For men, you commonly hear things like:

- "Did you hit that yet?"
- "Bro, did you get that yet?"

As if a woman's body is a prize to conquer, a trophy to collect, and a status booster.

For women, you commonly hear:

- "When are you going to give it up?"
- "If you don't sleep with him, someone else will and you'll lose him."

Look at how this culture has devalued something God designed to be covenantal, beautiful, and holy. Sex was never meant to be a transaction, a bargaining chip, or a "test drive."

These messages have trained us to believe that boundaries are restrictive, that purity is outdated, and that holding standards will cause you to miss out on love.

"Sex-Pectations"

As a Christian man or woman who is desiring a Godly relationship that leads to marriage you must live according to the word of God and aware of satans tricks, traps, and devices that we are not to be ignorant of (2 Cor. 2:11). One device of satan is the pressure and status offered by *cultural "Sex-Pectations."* This is the inbread expectation of sexual activity as the standard for status, and contentment. Family, it is warped. The age of first consensual sexual encounter is dipping lower and lower. In my experience, I have worked with a number of pre-teens and teens who have had documented more than 6 sexual partners. The youngest being only 12 years old. The most disturbing part is that they feel proud of what culture calls their **"Body Count"** — (the number of sexual partners) Just let that sink in. The majority of them are young girls who have been swept into a culture of lust, dishonoring and sinning against their own bodies (1 Cor. 6:18). Being in this world but not of it requires you to be "eyes wide open" to the Sex-pectations of anyone you meet. This includes being brave enough to choose your core and friend groups according.

> **"The most disturbing part is that they feel proud of what culture calls their Body Count"**

But what if?....

Understand this: If you have been misled by these cultural

influences and have crossed sexual boundaries, you are not disqualified from God's plan.

Maybe you crossed the line before. Maybe you believed the lie before. But this book is not meant to be just informational — it is transformational. Despite any mistakes, or bad choices you've made, you can choose to renew your mind about sexual boundaries today. From this moment forward, you can decide to honor God's covenant, God's design, and God's boundaries so you can build a healthy, purposeful relationship in the future.

Purity is not about perfection — it is about intention. It's about choosing to honor God with your body and your heart. It's about choosing to honor the person you are interested in, even if they don't end up as your spouse. It's about seeing every individual as precious, worthy, and deserving of respect and to be protected. The world says boundaries are about controlling you. But God says boundaries are about protecting you.

Why Sex Belongs in Marriage

Let me be clear. Sex is God's idea, and it is a good gift — but only in the right context. Hebrews 13:4 tells us: "Marriage is honorable among all, and the bed undefiled; but fornicators and adulterers God will judge." That means inside marriage, sex is blessed, safe, and holy. The marriage bed is undefiled — meaning it is pure before God.

But what does that say about unmarried people having sexual relationships? It means those sexual acts defile what God meant to be holy. They twist something designed for covenant into something casual, and they risk opening the door to emotional chaos, spiritual confusion, soul ties, shame, and regret.

"Remember, this book is for those who want to do relationships and marriage God's way."

The best way to do things God's way is to do things according to His word. So believe me when I say that honoring God with your body matters deeply. Don't just take my word. Take God's word.

1 Corinthians 6:18-20 says:

> "Flee sexual immorality. Every other sin a person commits is outside the body, but whoever sins sexually sins against their own body... You are not your own; you were bought at a price. Therefore, honor God with your bodies."

You don't own yourself — God does. He paid for you with the blood of Jesus Christ. Your body is His temple. Our purity is a form of worship, honor, and showing gratitude for God Almighty paying for us with the blood of His Son, Jesus. So protect yourself and prepare for a marriage that will be healthy, secure and trustworthy.

The Power of Sexual Sobriety

Although the noise of this culture, with its imagery, and push for sexual perverseness can seem dizzying, it only substantiates the need for sexual sobriety. Sexual sobriety is a powerful concept. It means making a daily, intentional commitment to walk in sexual purity, no matter the social cost and no matter your past.

Dr. Doug Weiss describes sexual sobriety as "a daily practice of honoring God with your sexuality, turning away from sexual impulses or habits that violate His best for your life." That is transformational!

It is not a daily practice of honoring peers' opinions, honoring the allure and pressure of eating from this culture's table of sexual sin. No! It's about daily purposing to honor God with your sexuality.

Here are some ways to practice Sexual Sobriety:

- **Setting boundaries**

Communication is Key. Be open about your decision for a sexually sober lifestyle.Any thought or feeling of Shame is the culture's Sex-pectation trying to bully you. Resist that.

- **Inviting accountability**

Seek a trustworthy mentor to check in with weekly about how you're managing your thought life and physical choices."

- **Staying honest with God**

If you feel tempted speak the word of God, and connect with your mentor, or safe, like minded community — instead of hiding or trying to handle it alone..

- **Being transparent with a safe, faith-filled and bible obeying community**

Share challenges and wins in your men's/women's group, knowing they'll speak truth and help you stay on track."

- **Refusing to let culture define what is your "normal"**

Resist culture's Sex-pectations knowing and believing that "Abstinence is not weird, it's not weak — for you, it's worship."

Sexual sobriety protects you from soul ties, spiritual confusion, emotional baggage, and bitterness that could sabotage your future marriage. Sex is a holy covenant act, not a casual experience.

This is why sexual sobriety and sexual wholeness matters.

Do This

1. Write down your non-negotiable purity boundaries.

_____
_____
_____
_____

2. List ways to communicate those boundaries clearly and early when dating.

_____
_____
_____
_____

3. Surround yourself with accountability — friends or mentors who will encourage your standards.

4. If you've crossed lines before, don't hide in shame. Bring it to God. Repent, reset, receive His grace, renew your mind with God's perspectives, and be transformed.

Pray This

"God, I thank You for giving me boundaries that protect me. You are a good father who always wants the highest and best for His children. I ask you to forgive me for complaining about your boudaries and standards and forgive me for crossing lines that dishonored You, me, and other individuals. Help me rebuild, walk in purity, and honor my future spouse — even before I meet them. Thank you for giving me the courage to uphold your relationship standards, no matter what culture says. I commit to honoring you with my body with a daily purpose to practice sexual sobriety.

In Jesus' name, amen."

Ponder This

- Where do I struggle with boundaries?

- What conversations do I need to have with future dating partners?

- How do I want to define purity for my life?

- Where did I first learn my ideas about sex, and how do I need to renew them with God's truth?

Journal This

- Where do I struggle with boundaries?

- What conversations do I need to have with future dating partners?

- How do I want to define purity for my life?

- Where did I first learn my ideas about sex, and how do I need to renew them with God's truth?

— JOURNAL YOUR RESPONSE BELOW —

-
-
-
-

Chapter 7
Big takeaway

> **"Enforcing My Boundaries & Proactive Purity -Are Acts of Worship- that protect my heart, my future, and my relationship with God."**

///////////////////////////////

Transformational Affirmation Decrees
for Boundaries, Purity, and Honor

"Take a moment to breathe and align yourself. This isn't about shame or perfection — it's about honoring God with your body, your boundaries, and your boldness. Culture may push you to blend in, compromise, or silence your convictions, but you were never called to follow the crowd. You were called to walk in covenant. Speak these truths with clarity, courage, and commitment."

1. I honor God with my body, my choices, and my boundaries.
2. I practice sexual sobriety as an act of daily worship and wisdom.
3. My worth supersedes culture, pressure, or past mistakes.
4. I reject compromise and choose covenant purity.
5. I set clear boundaries that protect my heart, mind, and spirit.
6. I am not my own — I was bought with a price, and I honor God with my life.
7. I stand firm on God's truth without conforming to culture's lies.
8. I walk in sexual integrity, accountability, and intentionality.
9. I am preparing for covenant love by living with honor today.
10. I let go of shame, and receive grace, and live as a whole, healed vessel of God.

"Family,

always remember — boundaries are not punishment. They are a divine security system for your purpose, your joy, and your future marriage. Don't allow the culture to talk you out of honoring God with your body and your heart.

You got this!"

///

Before you can fully love someone else, you've got to confront the places where Relationship & "Love Molds" first formed. In Chapter 8, we're diving into the often unspoken impact of your father and mother wounds. Whether your parents were present but emotionally unavailable, loving but broken, or absent altogether—their example planted seeds. Some grew into wisdom. Others into walls.

This chapter is not about blame — it's about breakthrough.

If you've ever caught yourself repeating generational patterns, choosing emotionally unavailable partners, or struggling to trust or receive love, this is your healing chapter. God doesn't just expose wounds and conditioning to shame you — He reveals them to so that you can receive the Healing that is already present for you.

Let's uproot the dysfunction and plant Kingdom seeds.

Chapter 8

Healing Father & Mother Wounds

Breaking Generational Cycles
Building Emotional & Relationship health

Let me ask you something real. Have you ever looked at the way you act in relationships and realized — "I'm just like my mom," or "I'm turning into my dad"? Whether you got along well with your parents or struggled with them, their patterns shape you. Sometimes for the better. Sometimes for the worse.

I grew up in a single-parent home. My father was not present. That left me with a wound I didn't even know I had — a wound that whispered, "Don't trust people. Be your own protector. Don't expect anyone to stay if times get tough. You must not be enough to stick around for." I carried that wound right into my relationships. I was always guarded, always suspicious, and way too quick to push people away. I developed the unique skill of making myself invisible in a relationship, knowing that it would cause a sense of separation to provoke my relationship partner to lose interest. That was my non-verbal, "it's not you-it's me" way to sabotage a relationship.

It wasn't until God showed me the root and the consequences of that fear, and helped me understand that I must allow my heart to be healed and my mind to be renewed, that I could truly open up and build something healthy. Understand that what you don't heal, you'll pass down — not just in marriage, but in the way you communicate, argue, withdraw, or even try to love.

> **"what you don't heal, you'll pass down"**

You might relate. Maybe your mom was emotionally unavailable. Maybe your dad was harsh or unpredictable. Maybe you saw chaos in their marriage.

Or maybe you grew up hearing your mother constantly complain about your father, degrade him, or tear him down. Hearing her repeat things like, "You don't need a man. You can do fine without a man." That belief took root in you, and you learned to guard yourself, to never depend on anyone, to never let a man lead, because you were taught that needing a man was a sign of weakness.

And brothers, maybe you were taught that emotions are weakness, or that women can't be trusted — and now it's hard for you to be vulnerable, or to lead with empathy and strength at the same time. Now, as an adult, you might notice that those beliefs are still subconsciously controlling your relationships, making it hard to trust, hard to partner, and hard to build with biblical unity.

Here's what I want you to know: Just because you came from dysfunction doesn't mean you have to repeat it.
But you do have to confront it.

Culture says, "That's just how I am." "Everyone struggles, so why bother?"

But ignoring a wound doesn't heal it. It only infects it. Some are reluctant to address their past because they fear they are dishonoring their upbringing, being ashamed of where they came from. But hear me, addressing and healing wounds doesn't dishonor your past. It honors your future.

Father and mother wounds can show up in all areas of life and are often accompanied by associated thoughts, feelings, and rationale such as:

- **Fear of abandonment or rejection**

"I always expect people to leave me, so I emotionally detach before they get too close."

- **Over-performing to earn love and acceptance**

"If I'm not excelling or being useful, I feel unworthy of love and attention."

- **Distrust of leadership or authority**

"I keep my guard up around pastors or mentors because I assume they'll disappoint or control me like my dad did."

- **Fear of conflict or deep connection**

"I avoid hard conversations because growing up, disagreement always led to yelling or silent treatment."

- **Resisting healthy submission or guidance**

"Even when someone's trying to help me grow, I push back — I don't like feeling like someone's over me."

Family, if you see yourself in any of the previous scenarios, remember your healing and transformation are as near as your choice to exchange and renew your beliefs and thinking about your past hurts. <u>Here are some action steps & tips:</u>

1. Confront those thoughts, Don't Ignore them

"Just because you came from dysfunction doesn't mean you have to repeat it. But confronting them are non-negotiable"

Ignoring wounds only deepens them. I encourage you to acknowledge the root, not suppress the symptoms. However, be careful and avoid addressing the wounding situation with complaints. Complaining brings attention to your wound but keeps the injury fresh. Rather, address the wound with gratitude for your healing and forgiveness for the perpetrator. It may sound and feel extreme. But it is the Biblical way. Forgiveness frees you from the weight and damage you have been carrying from the hurtful situation.

2. Receive Healing of the Wound, or past hurt

"God, I receive healing from every wound from my parents, parental figures, my past or my childhood."

I encouraged you to approach healing honestly and with faith that Jesus Christ has already endured the physical and psychological pain for you so that you may simply believe and receive the healing that he afforded you. Invite the Holy Spirit to help you be aware of any places of brokenness for healing and renewal. Understanding that the place of brokenness is connected to a painful belief from the past that needs to be replaced with a Healthy, empowering belief.

3. Commit to Breaking the Pattern

"Commit to a new pattern, even if you're the first in your family to do so."

I challenge you to make a different choice, to stop the cycle rather than pass it on. Remember that making a different choice is going to require you to renew your mind about the old pattern. When we put our emphasis on changing an act, we often overlook the cause of the act—our beliefs. Therefore, in order to break a habitual pattern of action, and to keep it broken we must change the way we think about that pattern of action. End the relationship of justifying that pattern of action and replace it with a new, healthy perspective.

4. Renew Your Mind with God's Truth

"Without mind renewal- Transforming your situations is impossible."

Renewing your mindset is vital. Romans 12:2 is the anchor — transformation comes by exchanging the meanings you assigned to your past hurts with God's Word, and building a new healthy belief system.

Mind Renewal Opportunity

Scripture tells us: "The Lord is near to the brokenhearted and saves the crushed in spirit." (Psalm 34:18)

As the song says, God is a "Good-Good Father." In fact, God is a perfect Father. He is nothing like anyone who failed you or hurt you. He wants you to heal those cracks in your heart so you can build a future on a solid foundation. He also promises that generational patterns can be broken. You do not have to repeat what you saw growing up. This is why we are on this journey together. It takes a renewed mind for any and every transformation. The fact that you are consuming this transformational book is evidence that you are here for a different outcome. You're here for Mind renewal and the transformation that is guaranteed. (Romans 12:2)

> **"A Renewed Mind is Required for any and every Transformation"**

Do This

1. Identify a wound you've carried from the past

   _____

   _____

2. Identify the meaning that you have assigned to the event or action that was hurtful.

   _____

   _____

3. Identify a scriptural promise from the Word of God that cancels out and replaces the meaning you have assigned that past hurt.

   _____

   _____

4. Write a forgiveness letter to them, even if you never send it
   Seek additional help & accountability via counseling, a pastor, a trusted mentor, or community
   Commit to a new pattern, even if you're the first in your family to do so

5. Speak this daily: "I forgive what I couldn't control, and am grateful for a healthy relationship future."

Pray This:

"Father God, I thank you for the healing power of Jesus Christ that is actively healing every wound from past. I humbly forgive everyone who has hurt me in any way. I renounce every offense that I have taken. I release them to Your best for their lives. I renounce every generational pattern in my family line that does not reflect Your love and Your truth. Help me to continually forgive, to release, and to rebuild on Your foundation. I trust you as the perfect Father in life.

In Jesus' name, amen."

Ponder This

- What was healthy about my parents' relationship model?
- What was unhealthy?
- Where do I see those patterns showing up in me?
- What does a healed, God-honoring pattern look like?

Journal This

- What was healthy about my parents' relationship model?

- What was unhealthy?

- Where do I see those patterns showing up in me?

- What does a healed, God-honoring pattern look like?

— JOURNAL YOUR RESPONSE BELOW —

-
-
-
-

Chapter 8
BIG TAKEAWAY

> "As I forgive those involved in my past hurts, I am healed from my family wounds"

> "Generational dysfunction may have run in the family —BUT IT STOPS WITH ME."

Transformational Affirmation Decrees

for Healing

Parental & Early Life Wounds

If we allow wounds from early life experiences to fester, they can shape how we see ourselves, trust others, and relate to God. But today, you take your power back. These decrees are not about blame; they are about breaking cycles and choosing healing. Speak them slowly. Speak them boldly. Let each truth become a brick in the foundation God is building in you — one of wholeness, identity, and unstoppable love

—Let's Go!

1. I confront past hurts with without blame, but in faith, and healing abounds in my soul.
2. I humbly forgive and renounce every offense I have taken.
3. I am free from my past — I am who God says I am.
4. I renounce every generational pattern that doesn't align with God's love and purpose for my life.
5. God's will determines my purpose.
6. I am free to love, trust, and connect in healthy, God-honoring ways.
7. God is my perfect Father — He has provided healing through Jesus Christ — I believe and receive it.
8. I choose new patterns that bless my future and my legacy.
9. My heart is open to love without fear because I am fully seen, safe, and secure in Christ.
10. I am the cycle-breaker — through God's truth and grace.

Family,

You are not stuck with the patterns you inherited. You are the cycle-breaker. You can build a legacy that looks nothing like the dysfunction you came from. And if you came from a healthy upbringing, use these transformational tools to position your relationship, marriage, and family for God's best.

God Almighty is equipping you to do just that.

Let's be real — independence is trendy, but isolation is dangerous. This world idolizes self-reliance and the myth of anyone being "Self-Made." It whispers, "You don't need anyone," which could not be further from the truth. You cannot address a weakness that you are not aware of. Blind spots are real and will sabotage the relationships pursued in isolation.

Relationship readiness happen in the context of trusted community. You need people who see you, check you, sharpen you, and hold you to your standards — especially when your emotions try to settle for less. In this chapter, we're breaking the lie that "me, myself, and I" is a success strategy. Real transformation requires real accountability. And the right circle? It doesn't just challenge you — it changes and prepares you.

Let's dive in.

Chapter 9

The Power of Accountability and Community

"Build a Godly support network to stay on track"

I get it — we live in this "do you" culture. "Stay in your lane." "Mind your business and trust no one." But can I be honest? That mindset will keep you stuck. You cannot grow alone. You cannot heal alone. And you cannot prepare for a healthy relationship alone.

Jason's Story

Jason was a strong, confident guy who had survived a hard childhood. He had been cheated on, lied to, abandoned — and he made up his mind that he'd never trust anyone again. He figured if he could keep everything private, stay to himself, and "handle it," he'd be safe and no one could hurt him. But guess what? Jason kept dating the same type of woman. He repeated the same patterns, fell for the same traps, and never really healed. Because when you only talk to yourself, you can only see what you already believe.

One day, Jason joined a men's group at his church. At first, he stayed silent. But then he opened up

— and that changed everything.

They challenged him. They prayed with him. The modeled truth and showed him blind spots. As a result, for the first time, he had accountability — real brothers who wouldn't let him slip back into old habits. Jason grew more in one year of *community* than he had in a whole decade of trying to "fix" himself alone.

In my own experience, I've seen the same power of community. When I became interested in my wife, Tangela, I had already begun working through my healing and mind renewal process. I had been taught the importance of having a solid, trustworthy community, and I felt confident about inviting Tangela into that space.

> "I made it a priority to connect her"

I made it a priority to connect her with my mentor, Dr. James D. Treadwell, Jr., and his wife, Deana Treadwell. As I was being sharpened and mentored by Dr. James, Tangela was also being sharpened and mentored, developing accountability with my trusted circle.

Beyond that, we intentionally surrounded ourselves with peers who had decades of healthy, joyful marriages. Because we were serious about a Godly marriage life that superceded what we saw in both of our family histories, we both limited our time with old friends who were driven by the culture we committed to leave. Instead, we chose a community of people who lived successful Godly marriages rather than reinforcing a broken cultural foundation.

One of the verses that kept us anchored during that time was Proverbs 11:14:

"Where no counsel is, the people fall: but in the multitude of counsellors there is safety."

It's important to note that this proverb doesn't mean you just consult with anyone. The counselors you choose should be wise, experienced, and capable of offering sound advice based on the Word of God and their fruit. Not just share their many failures. I'm telling you the truth. That may be good. But Good could be the Enemy of the Best that God has for you. Choose your counsel based on their Fruit.

"Choose your counsel based on their Fruit"

"Jesus said, You will know them by their Fruit Not Their Degree or Credentials"

This principle protected us from wrong turns and regretful outcomes. Wise, godly counsel builds you up — it doesn't push you into culture's hype. **Also, reflect on Proverbs 15:22 that teaches us:**

"Without counsel purposes are disappointed, but in the multitude of counsellors they are established."

This is how you build safety, security, and wisdom for your future.

Even today — going on 30 years of marriage — Tangela and I still spend time in our community, drawing from the collective wisdom of over 250 combined years of healthy, happy, God-honoring marriages. That circle has been a rock for us, helping us stay accountable, inspired, and committed to building something that lasts.

Monica's Story

Let me also tell you about **Monica** who had always struggled in relationships. Every relationship felt toxic, short-lived, or filled with drama. Trying to figure out what was wrong, she turned to social media, following popular "relationship gurus," podcasts, and influencers who basically just complained about their relationships, love, men, and marriage. It felt like everyone was angry and hopeless. The more Monica listened, the more negative she became. She was saturated and inundated with voices that were cynical, fearful, and critical of healthy commitment.

Then one day, a colleague at work — a Christian who believed in God's design for relationship and marriage overheard the programs, pulled Monica aside and told her something that changed everything:

"Monica, as long as you're listening to that kind of input, you'll never get the kind relationship that you really want."

That colleague invited Monica to learn a new way. They began sharing biblical truths about love, marriage, and purpose. They mentored her and prayed with her.

Over time, Monica's mindset changed. She healed from past

trauma, replaced bitterness with forgiveness, and built a healthy, godly, biblical view of love. Today, she is no longer chained to her old bitterness or fear. She is hopeful and wise about pursuing her future relationships. This transformation was not because of hype from social media relationship gurus who feed from culture, but because she has renewed her mind with God's truth and is walking forward in confidence.

Maybe you've felt like Jason. Maybe you've felt like Monica. Maybe you think no one needs to know your business, or you can do this whole relationship journey by yourself.

Family—Respectfully, you cannot. God designed you for connection. For community. For accountability. Proverbs 27:17 says: *"As iron sharpens iron, so one person sharpens another."*

> **"Isolation's false sense of security will fool you, but Community will refine you"**

Isolation's false sense of security will fool you, but Community will refine you.

God built the church for a reason. He wants you to have brothers and sisters, mentors, spiritual family — people who can challenge you, encourage you, and even correct you in love.
James 5:16 says
"Confess your sins to each other and pray for each other so that you may be healed."

> *Healing comes through confession*
> *— not hiding.*
> *Growth comes through community*
> *— not isolation.*

Do This

1: Identify two people you can trust to hold you accountable

Trustworthy accountability partners help anchor you in truth when your feelings try to lead you astray. (Determine if they are candidates to partner with you in numbers 2-4 Below)

- _____

- _____

2: Share your story — your challenges, your patterns, your goals

Transparency breaks the power of shame and invites others to support your growth with clarity, compassion, and specific scriptural interventions..

3: Meet regularly to pray, talk honestly, receive correction and direction.

Consistent connection keeps you aligned with God's path and prevents you from drifting into isolation or self-deception.

4: Stay teachable. Let others help you see the blind spots you can't see or are not willing to acknowledge on your own.

Teachability is the bridge between awareness and transformation — it opens the door to growth you couldn't access alone.

Pray This

"Father, thank You for designing me for community. I choose to reject isolation and pride. Give me courage to build healthy, trustworthy relationships that will hold me accountable, encourage me, and keep me grounded. Surround me with wise people who love You and want to see me grow.

In Jesus' name, amen."

Ponder This

- Who or What do I allow to speak into my life right now — Both positively and negatively?

- Do I have mentors and Kingdom friends, or am I isolated?

- Do I tend to Isolate myself? If so, Why?

- What could change if I allowed safe, godly people to help me grow?

Journal This

- Who or What do I allow to speak into my life right now — Both positively and negatively?

- Do I have mentors and Kingdom friends, or am I isolated?

- Do I tend to Isolate myself? If so, Why?

- What could change if I allowed safe, godly people to help me grow?

— JOURNAL YOUR RESPONSE BELOW —

-
-
-
-

Chapter 9
BIG TAKEAWAY

> "Transformation happens in community
> — not in isolation."
>
> "Accountability doesn't weaken you
> — it strengthens you and is the cheat-code
> for Your Relationship Future."
>
> "As I walk with the Wise
> — I Become Wise"
> Proverbs 13:20

Transformational Affirmation Decrees
for Accountability & Community

Transformation and healing for healthy relationships doesn't happen in secrecy or in the dark. It happens in the light of godly relationships, in safe spaces where love tells the truth and iron sharpens iron. Healing was never meant to be a solo journey. As you declare these affirmations, open your heart to the power of connection.

God is not just healing you — He's aligning you with the right people to walk with you. Speak these words as a seed being planted in the soil of your heart.

1. I grow best in Godly community — isolation is no longer my safe space.
2. I invite wise, loving accountability into my journey because I was not created to heal alone.
3. I am surrounded by voices that sharpen, not shame me.
4. I reject the lie that privacy equals protection — I choose truth, trust, and transparency.
5. I welcome correction from those anchored in God's Word, because correction brings wisdom.
6. I am open, honest, and accountable with faith-filled mentors who speak life into me.
7. I choose my community based on the God given purpose for my life.
8. My transformation is deepened through connection, not control.
9. I renounce offenses, pride and isolation and I welcome edifying relationships.
10. God is placing the right people around me to help me grow, stay grounded, and thrive.

Family,

Please hear me — isolation feels safe, but isolation alone will never build you. God made you to walk this out together. So go get your community, and let them sharpen you.

There are not many life challenges that test character more than having to wait for something you desire— waiting can be tough. Especially when you feel like everyone else is living your dream.

But what if God's delay is actually His divine development?

What if the timeline you're wrestling with isn't a punishment, but a setup for something greater than you imagined?

In this chapter, we're going to confront the pressure of earthly timelines and exchange it for the peace and safety of God's perfect timing. You'll learn how to trust Him when it feels like nothing is happening — and discover that, behind the scenes, He's preparing everything... including you. Don't let the clock dictate your confidence.

— Let God be the Engineer of your timeline —

CHAPTER 10

God's Timing versus Your Timeline

"God's timing is not late — it's perfect, precise, and intentional."

It is prevalent in society to feel like you're "running out of time." Maybe you're watching friends get married, posting baby announcements, living the dream — and you're sitting there wondering: "Lord... did You forget about me?" If you've ever felt behind, please hear me: God has not forgotten you. He is not ignoring you. He is preparing you.

Kiera's Story

Let me tell you about Kiera, a twenty-six-year-old, beautiful, smart, and strong in her faith woman. But year after year, she watched her friends walk down the aisle, and she started to panic. She prayed, but secretly, she worried God was moving too slow. So when someone finally showed up — he looked good, talked good, said he loved God —

"So she jumped in fast."

They dated for four months before getting engaged. Everyone celebrated. But something deep inside Kiera didn't feel right. She pushed it down, because finally, she was going to be a bride. Six months before the wedding, everything crumbled. She found out he was unfaithful, controlling, and living a double life. Her heart was shattered. **Kiera had confused fast for blessed.** She thought God was late, so she took control.

Maya's Story

And then there was Maya. Maya was thirty-five when she met her husband. She'd spent her twenties and early thirties growing, healing, building her relationship with God, learning to love her singleness. People tried to rush her:

"You're getting older!"

"Aren't you worried about your biological clock?"

But Maya kept trusting God. When she finally met Marcus, their values lined up perfectly. Their faith was strong. Their friendship was solid.

Was it quick? — No.
But, was it worth it? — Absolutely.

Family hear me, God is never late. He's the God of perfect timing.

He will not release you into a relationship until you're ready — and until the other person is ready. Remember, He is the best father and wants the best for you — his child.

While Culture screams:

"IF YOU DON'T HURRY YOU'LL MISS YOUR CHANCE!"

God says:

"**Commit your plans to the Me** [submit and trust them to Me], **and your plans will succeed** [if you respond to My will and guidance]".

(Proverbs 16:3)

Will and Tangela's Story

Let me share my own experience with you.

When Tangela and I were in pre-marital counseling, we went through deep mentoring, accountability, and relationship training with our mentors. They helped us work through our blind spots, past hurts, family and cultural conditioning, develop our skills, and get prepared for a marriage built on God's principles. Eventually, they asked us to pick a wedding date. After praying and talking it through, we chose August 19th, 1995, and everyone agreed it sounded good. We began notifying family, setting plans, and getting excited. I also secured an apartment that was on hold until after the wedding.

But about a month before the wedding, my mentor, Dr. James D. Treadwell Jr., called us into his office. He asked us to consider pushing the wedding date back. We didn't argue or question it — we simply trusted his wisdom and trusted that God was guiding us through him. So we started looking for other dates and suggested February of 1996, which would have delayed the wedding by six months. Dr. James responded in his signature, God acknowledging pause: "Hmmmmm, Nah, it doesn't have to be that far off. Just move that date out of August." We trusted him and did just that. We settled on *October 28, 1995.*

"We trusted that God was Guiding us through him"

Here's the crazy part:

On August 27th, 1995, a massive fire broke out and burned down an entire section of the development, including the exact unit we were to live in.

I need to make sure you are tracking here. If we had stuck with our original wedding date, we might have been asleep in that apartment the night of the fire. Even if we were not home, we would have lost every single thing we owned.

That experience taught me a lesson I will never forget: God's timing is always best. It is not just about convenience — it is about your protection, your safety, and making sure every detail around you is prepared for your success.

"Beware of Leadership & Authority Phobias "

Avoidant attachment styles, past hurts, and even the "rumor-mill can land you in a self-sabotaging space where your heart becomes hardened to human counsel, advice and direction for fear of being lead astray, deceived, or taken advantage of. Please understand, that God primarily speaks to us through HIS word spoken through a human vessel. Don't fall pray to leadership and authority phobias. They can cripple you in all aspects of life.

Therefore, when God — and godly mentors who love you — ask you to wait, they're not trying to hold you back from a good thing. They're trying to set you up for blessing, peace, safety, and relationship success..

> *"Delayed does not mean Denied.*
> *It means*
> *God is Preparing something that can carry the weight of HIS purpose"*

Mind Renewal Opportunity

Galations 6:9 says:

"And let us not grow weary of doing good, for in due season we will reap, if we do not give up."

Be encouraged to be strong in your single-season understanding that using this time to prepare and renew your mind can only result in you obtaining the Godly relationship you desire. Never give up in your preparation.

Our timelines are often not the same as God's timeline. And that's okay because every season of waiting is a chance to grow, heal, mature, and get ready for what's coming.

"God's timing is not late

— it's perfect, precise, and intentional."

Do This

1: Write down 3 things you feel "late" concerning.

- _____
- _____
- _____

2: List 3 benefits of the season you're in right now

- _____
- _____
- _____

3: List 3 things God is teaching you personally as you are engaged in this book.

- _____
- _____
- _____

4: Have a humble (2-way) conversation with your Heavenly Father about your timeline, and surrender it back to HIM. (What was HIS reply?)

_____
_____
_____
_____
_____
_____

Pray This

"Lord, thank You for perfect timing. Forgive me when I get impatient or fearful. Strengthen my heart to trust You. Help me focus on who I'm becoming instead of what I think I'm missing. I believe Your plan for me is good, and I will wait in faith.

In Jesus' name, amen."

///////////////////////////////////

Ponder This

In what ways have I been comparing my journey to the journey of others?

Reflect on Kiera's story; are there ways that you relate?

Reflect on Maya's story; are there ways that you relate?

How do I want to use my waiting season to grow?

Reflect on Will and Tangels's story, In what ways can you see God is protecting you through a time of waiting?

Journal This

- **In what ways have I been comparing my journey to the journey of others? How has this comparison impacted my peace, perspective, or relationship decisions?**

  Journal how God might see your journey differently. What truth from His Word renews your mind in this area?

- **As I Reflect on Kiera's story; are there ways that you relate? What similar thoughts, emotions, or silent frustrations have I carried in my own waiting season?**

  Now compare: What would God say about this season you're in? What does His Word offer as a new lens for you to see it through?

- **How do I want to use my waiting season to grow? List two intentional ways I can invest in my personal, spiritual, or emotional development right now.**

  Invite God into your growth plan—ask Him to highlight what He wants to strengthen in you during this time. What mindsets need to shift?

- **As I Reflect on Will and Tangela's story; in what ways can I see God protecting me through a time of waiting? Are there doors God may have closed or delays He allowed that now make sense in hindsight?**

  Ask the Holy Spirit to show you what He shielded you from. What new gratitude or understanding does this bring to your heart and mind?

—JOURNAL YOUR RESPONSE BELOW—

-
-
-
-

Big takeaway

> "God's timing is better than my timeline because He is considering my safety, peace, and overall well-being."

Transformational Affirmation Decrees to cooperate with God's Timing vs. My Timeline

Remember, You are not behind — you are becoming. God's timing is not a delay; it's divine design. Every moment of waiting is shaping you for the promise. As you speak these affirmations, let go of fear, comparison, and control. Step into trust. God is not making you wait to punish you — He's preparing you to prosper.

Let's go!

1. I trust God's timing over my own because He sees what I cannot see.
2. I am on time — I am in process, and God is preparing me for something great.
3. I release fear and comparison; my path is custom-designed by God.
4. I commit my plans to the Lord, and I trust He will establish every step (Proverbs 16:3).
5. I will remain strong in doing the right thing, for in due season I will reap if I do not give up (Galatians 6:9).
6. God has not forgotten me — He is setting the stage for something better than I imagined.
7. I am using this waiting season to grow, heal, and become ready for what's coming.
8. I will not confuse speed with blessing — I trust that God is both intentional and protective.
9. Delays are not denials — they are divine redirections for my safety and success.
10. My faith is in God's perfect plan, and I choose to wait with purpose, peace, and praise.

Family,
I know it can be challenging to wait. I know the clock sounds loud sometimes. But trust me — one day you'll look back and thank God for every moment He told you to slow down. I am a personal witness that you'll see He was writing a better relationship story than you ever imagined.

Culture will tell you to follow your feelings. But feelings can be fickle, and chemistry doesn't equal covenant.

As you grow in purpose and maturity, it's not enough to just want a relationship — you've got to be able to discern one. Discernment is the God-given ability to sense what's truly from Him — not just what looks good, sounds good, or feels right in the moment. It's not just about avoiding the wrong relationship — it's about recognizing the right one when it shows up.

In Chapter 11, we'll break down how to sharpen your spiritual discernment during your preparation season. You'll learn how to filter charm through character, emotion through alignment, and excitement through truth. This is your time to grow in vision, clarity, and the confidence that only comes when your heart is surrendered and your mind is renewed.

Decide to stop letting culture decide for you — and start letting the Holy Spirit — through "the Word of God" take Lead.

Chapter 11

Discerning Right Relationships

"Using Biblical Wisdom to Evaluate Character for
Kingdom Compatibility"

*L*et's talk about something that trips a lot of us up: discernment. Most of us have learned to look for a spark, a vibe, a connection. But that alone can be dangerous if you don't have discernment. Because let's be honest — chemistry can lie. And feelings can trick you.

Lisa's Story

Lisa was a smart, passionate, God-fearing woman in her early thirties. She prayed for a husband and finally met a guy who swept her off her feet. He was charming, fun, and said all the right things. But something felt...off.

He dodged questions about his past. He was avoidant, defensive and skeptical about spiritual things, such as church and believing that the bible is truly the word of God. Lisa's friends tried to wave red flags, but she ignored them because *"this feels so good."* Six months in, she found out he was still seeing other women.

Heartbroken, Lisa realized her desire to be chosen had blinded her to the truth.

Anthony's Story

Then there was **Anthony**, a ministry youth leader who had been single for years, frustrated but prayerful. When he met Simone, everything looked good on paper. She was beautiful, involved in church, and seemed genuine.

But Anthony decided to do something different: He slowed down. He asked questions. He invited trusted mentors to meet her.

Over time, little inconsistencies started surfacing. She seemed jealous of his ministry commitments. She wanted to pull him away from his purpose. Anthony realized that this is a distraction, not a destiny partner. It stung to walk away, but a year later, God connected him with a woman who not only loved him but loved the mission God had placed on his life.

> **Family listen,**
> **"Your feelings are important**
> **—but they are not the final authority."**

Discernment protects you from repeating heartbreak.

<u>Discernment says:</u>

"I will look for their fruit."
"I will invite trusted voices."
"I will test what they say against what they do."

The Bible says in 1 John 4:1: *"Beloved, do not believe every spirit, but test the spirits to see whether they are from God…"*

Test their spirit. Test their fruit. Test their patterns.

Let's break down what discernment really is. *Discernment is the ability to judge well; to see beyond the surface; to recognize what is healthy and what is unhealthy, what is true and what is false.*

<u>Other words that help you understand discernment include:</u>

- **Wisdom**
- **Insight**
- **Spiritual perception**
- **Good judgment**
- **Clarity**
- **Prudence**
- ***God-given sense from the Bible**

This is not the culture's common sense that has been dramatically tainted. Jesus said, in the last days culture would call what is right-wrong, and what is wrong-right. We would lean towards what is against God and lean away from God's preferences. To better help you understand "God-given sense" from the bible, lets look at Stephanie's story.

Stephanie's Story: God-Given Sense on Display

Stephanie had been dating Mark for five months. On paper, everything seemed right. He had a great job, attended church, and said he believed in God. Her friends were impressed because her phone stayed lit up with heart emojis and sweet messages. But something kept nagging her. She remembered what her mentor once told her, "Don't just go by vibes. Go by the Word." So Stephanie began filtering her relationship through Scripture. When Marcus pressured her to move in before marriage, she remembered *Hebrews 13:4 — "Marriage should be honored by all and let the marriage bed be undefiled, for God will judge the sexually immoral..."*

When he avoided accountability and spiritual conversations from mature Christian men, she thought of *Proverbs 11:14-"Where there is no counsel, the people fall."* And when he consistently put his preferences before her boundaries, she recalled *1 Corinthians 13:5 that says "True Love is not self-seeking..."*

That was her God-given sense from the bible. It isn't a loud voice, not a lightning bolt, but the gentle wisdom of God's Word rising up as her guiding compass.

"Discernment helps you separate facts from feelings, fruit from mere words..."

The Word of God had spoken. She ended the relationship, not out of anger, but with peace. Because she wasn't just looking for love. She was walking in discernment and using God's Word as her manual. And in doing so, she didn't just protect her heart—she positioned her future.

Family, discernment is like heavenly sight into experiences through Heaven's eyes. Discernment helps you separate facts from feelings, fruit from mere words, reality from wishes, and illusions. It keeps you from being distracted by the sparks of "chemistry" while missing the indicators of true character.

This culture struggles with that. It preaches *"accept everyone as they are, no matter what,"* and calls that love. It calls it being fair

> **"This Culture Pressures you to adopt Radical Inclusivity without asking healthy questions or should I say, 'Heavenly Questions.'"**

Culture wants you to silence your spiritual instincts and feel guilty for noticing red flags.

But God's Word shows us that while we are called to love everyone, we are **not** called to align with everyone. Discernment is your safeguard. You can love people and pray for them, but you do not have to build a future with them.

Jesus said, "You will know them by their fruit." That means what you *see* consistently over time — not just what you feel in a moment — is the real evidence of their character. Discernment gives you the courage to look beyond someone's potential and pay attention to their patterns. It empowers you to separate the *vibe* from the *evidence* and the sweet talk from the lived truth.

Understand this:
Even if someone has issues, discernment helps you see whether their heart is open to God for true transformation. If they are genuinely surrendering, growing, and renewing their mind, that is far different from someone who is stuck, unrepentant, and unwilling to change.

Family, I want you to see something even bigger here.

This chapter — and *every* chapter in this book — is about developing your discernment. From renewing your relationship blueprint, to healing trauma bonds, to challenging cultural beliefs, every lesson has been strengthening your spiritual eyesight. Godly discernment is like a muscle. The more you practice separating His truth from the world's messages, the stronger and clearer you become. This discernment requires you to grow up in our relationship, understanding and let go of childish culture-laced perspectives. With maturity, you must build your relationship muscles in God's gym by repetitiously using HIS word as your compass, gauge, and guideline.

"But solid food is for the [spiritually] mature, whose senses are trained by practice to distinguish between what is morally good and what is evil." (Hebrews 5:14).

Every step you have taken through these chapters has helped you break away from culture's broken ideas so you can stand firmly in the Kingdom of God's wisdom. You are becoming someone who can tell the difference between what you *truly* desire and what the world tries to pressure you to settle for.

This is not just about gaining information and reading someone's mail. Rather, this is *Kingdom discernment* and a renewed mind that empowers you to build your future on a solid foundation, not a shifting cultural trend.

Keep sharpening it. Keep practicing it. And remember:
The Kingdom of God's wisdom will always look different than the world's hype.

Jesus said you will know a tree by its fruit (Matthew 7:16).
Look beyond words. Look beyond chemistry. Look at the character. Look at consistency.

Look at how they treat *everyone*, not just you. Because the way you treat anyone is the way you treat everyone, given the right trigger being pushed. Discernment is a gift from God, and you *can* grow it through prayer, studying God's perspectives from the Word, wise counsel, and slowing down.

This will help you to overcome one of This Age's biggest enablers of relationship and family destruction—**the "Feelings."**

Feelings versus Discernment

The American Psychological Association defines feelings as a self-contained phenomenal experience. Feelings are subjective, evaluative, and independent of the sensations, thoughts, or images evoking them. They are inevitably evaluated as pleasant or unpleasant.

Let's unpack this:

"Feelings"

Feelings are **"YOUR" personal,** inner responses to what you experience — kind of like the emotional "temperature" inside you. They are shaped by the Meaning you attach to any past or current situation or experience. The meaning you attach determines what you believe about the experience and all other experiences that appear the same "to you." What you believe determines what you think—and what you think dictates what you will feel. So, your feelings don't always come from truth, nor from facts. Face the fact that your feelings don't always make sense, but they are real to you. You might feel good or bad, excited or uneasy — even if the experience that triggered it doesn't fully explain why. That's because **Your feelings are personal to you**, and they show up based on how you've been conditioned, shaped, what you value, and even what you've been through.

It's important to pay attention to feelings, but also to recognize that although feelings are a real experience, they are not reliable or trustworthy unless they are triggered by the Word of God — the Absolute Truth.

"Discernment"

Discernment is the God-given ability to perceive truth beyond appearances. It's not just about knowing right from wrong — it's about knowing what is God's will versus what just feels right in the moment.

In relationships, discernment helps you filter through charm, chemistry, and charisma to see the fruit, the character, and the spiritual alignment. It's a function of a renewed mind and a surrendered heart — sharpened by prayer, scripture, wise counsel, and the Holy Spirit.

> **Discernment is the ability to view experiences, behaviors, and functionality through the light of God's Word.**

Consider discernment like the Ultraviolet lights detectives use in crime shows. You've seen the light scanners that can be used to detect blood or other evidence when it can't be detected by the naked eye. Discernment is the ability to view experiences, behaviors, and functionality through the light of God's Word. Superimposing the scripture onto your dealings takes practice, but I promise you this: it will mature you and strengthen you ability to discern properly.

The diagram below will help you to understand the contrasting operations of Feelings vs. Biblical Discernment

Feelings — versus —	Discernment
Driven by emotions, chemistry, and desire in the moment	Guided by the Word, the Spirit, wisdom, and fruit inspection over time
Feels urgent and reactive ("I feel it, so it must be right")	Responds with patience and clarity ("Let me see what's really here")
Can be clouded by past wounds or unmet needs	Filters through God's truth, not personal history

Do This:

1: List 2 non-negotiables of a godly partner

- _____
- _____

2: Ask trusted mentors to give honest feedback about someone you're considering

3: Observe how prospectives handle stress, conflict, and correction.

Journal This

- Where have I let feelings override red flags?

- Who can help me see clearly?

- What does a healthy, godly partner look like to me?

- List 2 Biblical Scriptures you believe can be used to superimpose onto your relationship experiences as "Ultraviolet Light" to see what your feelings may try to ignore.

—JOURNAL YOUR RESPONSE BELOW—

-
-
-
-

Chapter 11
BIG TAKEAWAY

> *"Discernment is my safeguard. The Word of God is my Measuring Tool"*

Transformational Affirmation Decrees
for Discerning the Right Relationship

Family, your heart is too valuable to gamble on vibes and surface attractions. Discernment is your divine safeguard and spiritual filter that protects you from deception, distraction, and desperation. As you declare these affirmations, you are strengthening your ability to see, hear God clearly, and choose wisely.

This is not just about hunting for red flags, but it is about honoring your worth, inviting God into your process, and building a future rooted in peace, truth, and purpose.

Let's declare God's wisdom over your relationships.

1. I am committed to pursuing peace in all situations. (Hebrews 12:14)

2. I trust God to reveal the truth behind charm, chemistry, and conversation.

3. I slow down, seek wise counsel, and observe fruit over time.

4. I am worthy of truth, peace, and alignment.

5. My feelings are real, but God's Word is final.

6. I reject counterfeit connections and make room for God's best.

7. I listen to the Holy Spirit and allow peace to confirm my steps.

8. I walk in wisdom and spiritual clarity.

9. I am a discerning builder, choosing character over hype.

10. I declare Matthew 7:16 over my life — I will know them by their fruit, not their performance.

Family,

Let me remind you — God is faithful to reveal truth if you slow down and ask Him. Feelings fade, but fruit stands the test of time. Let discernment be your guardrail. You deserve the right relationship, not just any relationship.

In Chapter 12, we bring everything full circle. Because the truth is, marriage readiness isn't about perfection — it's about maturity, identity, and alignment. It's about who you're becoming long before you say "I do." God doesn't waste the waiting season — He uses it to anchor you in truth, shape your character, heal your heart, and build a foundation that can withstand the weight of covenant.

You'll learn what it means to be spiritually grounded, emotionally secure, and relationally intentional. Not waiting idly — but building actively.

Because family,

God's purposes for marriage are too vital to prepare for passively.

Let's make sure that what you're building now is strong enough to hold what you're praying for later.

Chapter 12

Becoming Marriage Ready Whole, Healed & Anchored

Bringing it all together for a "Purposefilled", God-honoring relationship

Family, you have walked through an incredible journey. You've confronted your patterns. You've challenged your thoughts. You've renewed your mind. Now let's talk about what it really means to be marriage ready.

Marriage readiness doesn't mean you're flawless. It means you're whole.

It means you know who you are, who you belong to, and why you're here. It means you're walking in mind renewal and healing. You're anchored in truth.

It means you're willing to keep growing, even after you find "the one" or are found by "the one" and say— "I do."

Jordan's Story

Let me tell you about Jordan. Jordan had grown up thinking marriage would fix everything. That once he had a ring on his finger, the insecurities would disappear, the wounds would magically heal, and life would finally make sense. But Jordan did the work. He spent time learning to know himself, to face his fears, to break free of generational patterns. He learned what healthy love looked like, what boundaries looked like, what wholeness felt like.

> "He learned what healthy love looked like, what boundaries looked like, what wholeness felt like."

By the time Jordan met someone who was aligned with his values, Jordan was ready — not because he was perfect, but because he was accountable and anchored. When conflict came up in dating, Jordan didn't spiral. When fear whispered old lies, Jordan had biblical truth to stand on. When things got challenging, Jordan understood how to approach them with faith in the word of God, and a community to lean on.

That's what readiness looks like. Not perfection. Not a highlight reel. But a healed, growing, anchored heart. Maybe you're like Jordan. Maybe you've spent years thinking "I'll be ready once I fix everything.

> *"Hear me — you will never be perfect in culture's terms. But you can be mature, healed and whole.*

You can walk into a marriage-prepping relationship as someone who knows how to forgive, releasing past offenses and choosing grace over resentment so that love can flow freely without hidden bitterness. You know how to communicate, express your needs, hear your partner's heart, all while navigating challenges with clarity and compassion. You will pray, acknowledging God as the lynchpin and authority in your relationship who covers your union with wisdom, strength, and peace beyond understanding. You'll continue to heal, acknowledging wounds without shame and allowing God's truth to rebuild the broken places in you and your relationship. You will love, not just with emotion but with commitment, sacrifice, patience, and service that mirrors the love of Christ. And finally, you commit to continually grow, remaining teachable, humble, and anchored in your personal development so that your future marriage doesn't just survive — it thrives.

That is the best gift you will ever give your future spouse.

Transformational Reminder

Family, everything you've read and worked through in this book was not purposed to be just informational. It was purposed to be transformational.

God wants you to experience true transformation — a renewed mind that empowers you to step into marriage as a whole, healed, healthy individual.

Romans 12:2 says:

"Do not conform to the patterns of this world, but be transformed by the renewing of your mind."

Every principle, every story, every reflection in these chapters has been designed to help you renew your thinking. Because a renewed mind will transform your heart, your habits, and your entire perspective and approach to relationships.

> "...a renewed mind will transform your heart, your habits — your entire perspective and approach to relationships."

That is **how you become truly marriage-ready.**

Mind Renewal Opportunity

Marriage is not about completing you — it's about partnering with you. God doesn't expect you to have zero flaws. He expects you to be humble, teachable, and anchored in Him and willing to renew your perspectives and mindsets to align with His.

Jesus says in Matthew 7:24:

"Everyone who hears these words of mine and puts them into practice is like a wise man who built his house on the rock."

You are building your life on the Rock. That is why your house — your marriage — will stand.

Do This

1: Keep investing in personal growth — therapy, mentoring, learning

—Example: Schedule monthly sessions with a pastor, counselor or life coach to work through unresolved issues or blind spots.

*Outcome: You'll enter marriage as a self-aware, emotionally balanced individual, who does not drag unprocessed baggage into your union.

2: Develop spiritual disciplines: prayer, worship, Scripture
—*Example:* Start each day with a time of prayer and Bible reading, asking God to shape your character and guide your choices.(Remember, Prayer is a "Two-Way" conversation)
Outcome: You'll become spiritually anchored, making decisions from a place of peace and discernment rather than pressure or emotion.

3: Create a vision for your marriage with God's purpose & values at the core
—*Example:* With Holy Spirit partnership; Journal your values for family, Committment to God, finances, and purpose, then decree, and communicate them regularly in trusted circles.

Outcome: You'll be able to recognize a compatible partner and avoid counterfeits that don't align with God's plan for your future.

4: Commit to continual check-ins, even after you're married
—*Example:* Establish a habit of "heart talks" with your spouse-to-be, and commit to premarital and post-marital check-ins with mentors.
Outcome: You'll build a culture of honesty, accountability, and growth — keeping your marriage healthy & strong long after the honeymoon ends.

Pray This:

"Lord, thank You for bringing me this far. I thank You for continuing the work you are doing in me. Im being Anchored in Your truth. My mind is being renewed . Thank you for grace to carry everything I've learned into my future marriage, so that I can love well, serve well, and reflect Your glory in my family.

In Jesus' name, amen."

Journal This

- What has changed in me during this process?

- In what areas do I still need Mind Renewal?

- What is something about me that could be a Red Flag or barrier to successful healthy relationship and Marriage?

- How will I continue to grow and protect my wholeness after I marry?

–JOURNAL YOUR RESPONSE BELOW–

-
-
-
-

Chapter 12
BIG TAKEAWAY

"Marriage readiness is not about perfection, but about being healed, whole, and anchored in God's truth through a renewed mind."

—

"God's preparation leads to lasting partnership."

—

"I can't just pray for the right person"

—

I must continue to become the person who's ready."

—

"Marriage readiness is about who I am becoming—not just who I am waiting for"

Transformational Affirmations Decrees for Being Marriage Ready

As you declare these final affirmations, remember you are not becoming "marriage material" later — you are being shaped now. You've broken cycles, renewed your mind, and learned to walk in truth. These declarations will anchor your identity, affirm your wholeness, and align your soul with the type of covenant love God desires for you to carry. Speak them out boldly — you are not behind, you are being built.

1. I am whole, healed, and anchored in God's truth.

2. I am actively being prepared and am surrendered and growing.

3. I am no longer waiting to be "fixed" — I am walking in freedom and wholeness now.

4. My identity is secure in Christ and I am prime for a Godly relationship and marriage.

5. I bring peace and purpose into every relationship I enter.

6. I am committed to growth and healing — before and after I say "I do."

7. I build my relationship blueprint on the rock of God's word. (Matthew 7:24)

8. I've renewed my mind, and I walk in God's wisdom, and am free from culture's confusion. (Romans 12:2)

9. I am ready to love, communicate, and lead with grace and strength.

10. I am committed to continued mind renewal so my future marriage will reflect God's glory.

Closing Prayer

"Father,

Thank You for walking with me through every chapter, every lesson, and every challenge on this journey. Thank You for exposing the lies I once believed, and for leading me to renew my mind, as You are rebuilding me from the inside out.

Lord, I ask You to continue to secure me by Your word, to strengthen my heart, and to anchor my life in Your truth. Help me to carry forward everything I've learned — into my relationships, my future marriage, and my family legacy.

Give me the grace, strength, and courage to walk in wholeness, to love with Your love, and to stand firm in Your Kingdom principles no matter what culture dictates. I thank you for Protecting me from deception. I welcome you to guide my steps. I thank you for surrounding me with a strong community of accountability.

I trust You, Father God, with my future. I trust You with my relationships. And I trust You with my purpose.

May my life, my love, my marriage and family legacy bring You glory.

In Jesus' name, amen."

Family,

If you've read this far, you've done something most people never do — you've invested in renewing your mind and reshaping your relationship future. You've looked in the mirror of God's Word, you've asked hard questions, and you've committed to becoming a whole, healed, and purposeful individual before you step into marriage.

I want you to know — you are not the same person who started this book. The patterns you've uncovered, the lies you've confronted, the truths you've embraced... these are the building blocks of a brand-new foundation. A foundation built on the Rock, not the shifting sands of culture.

You now know how to:

- *Examine and renew your relationship blueprint so it aligns with God's truth.*

- *Distinguish culture's lies from Kingdom wisdom in how you date and prepare for marriage.*

- *Value wholeness before oneness, healing before joining hearts.*

- *Recognize and reject the Fix-It Syndrome so you can love from a place of strength, not survival.*

- *Pursue God's timing over your own and trust His preparation process.*

- *Walk in discernment so you can identify the right relationships and avoid the wrong ones.*

- *Commit to covenant-level love, not convenience-based connections.*

But here's the thing — knowledge alone isn't transformation. Transformation happens when you take what you've learned and live it daily.

So I challenge you:

Keep speaking the transformational decrees you've learned in this book.

Keep doing the journal work.

Keep checking your heart against the Word of God.

Keep surrounding yourself with a Kingdom community that will hold you accountable.

You are not "waiting" for a godly marriage — you are preparing for one. Every choice you make now, every boundary you set, every time you honor God with your heart and actions — you are laying bricks for a future that will last.

I'll leave you with this:
Don't just pray for the right person — become the person who's ready.
Your preparation is not wasted. Your wholeness is your witness. And your obedience to God's timing will produce a love story that brings Him glory.

Let's keep building — together.

— Coach Will Lane

— Call to Action —

You have come this far, and I want to challenge you not to stop here. Transformation doesn't end on the last page of a book. It continues in the way you live from here on out.

You are called to build a life and legacy that honors God, and it starts right now with these tools.

— Family Success Solutions Assessments —

S.W.A.G. Assessment (for Singles):

<u>*Single with a Goal Assessment*</u> to Discover your emotional, spiritual, & relational readiness for a purposeful, God-centered relationship.

Scan or Click here to take the Free Assessment

S.W.A.G. Assessment

M.R.R.A. Assessment (for Couples):

<u>**The Marriage Readiness-Relationship Alignment Assessment**</u> helps pre-marriage couples and married couples gain insight into their alignment, communication, and growth areas as a couple—whether they're still preparing for marriage or strengthening the one they are in.

Scan or Click here to take the Free Assessment

M.R.R.A. Assessment

— Call to Action —

Book Coaching Sessions

1. "Need 1-on-1 support?" [virtual]

Book a session with Coach Will Lane to break cycles, build clairty, renew your mind and walk in alignment.

2. "Apply for Relationship Coaching" [virtual]

If you're ready to take real action, apply for coaching sessions with you and your partner

3. "Group Coaching" [virtual]

Join a live group coaching experience and grow with others who are serious about healing, growth, and doing relationships God's way.

4. "Book A Live Workshop for Your Group"

[Live-in person]

Subscribe to the Family Success Solutions Youtube Channel

—Watch transformational teachings, interviews, and live coaching sessions.

https://rebrand.ly/wb3f3k1

Follow the Success & Family Podcast

— Get wisdom and strategies to build godly, purpose-filled relationship and family tips.

https://rb.gy/3m8edm

Your future is too important to leave to chance.

God has already planted seeds of transformation in you through this book — now water them, nurture them, and watch Him grow something amazing in your life.

I am so proud of you, and I'm cheering you on

Let's build Kingdom relationships and Heal families

together from the inside Out.
— Coach Will

Relationship Affirmation Decree Vault

Chapter 1 Decrees

1. I am whole, valuable, and complete in Christ in my season of singleness.

2. My single season is filled with purpose, preparation, and growth.

3. I choose to build a strong, godly foundation for my future.

4. I honor God with how I use this time to heal, mature, and develop.

5. I am being prepared for a purpose-filled relationship that reflects God's design.

6. I am right on time in God's plan for me.

7. I invest in my personal growth and allow God to shape my character.

8. I embrace God's perspective and reject the lies of culture.

9. I attract healthy relationships by becoming emotionally and spiritually whole.

10. I walk confidently in my identity, knowing God is writing my story with wisdom and love.

Chapter 2 Decrees

1. I am renewing my mind daily and building my relationship life on God's truth.

2. I release every toxic belief I inherited and embrace God's design for love and unity.

3. I break inner vows that no longer serve my healing or purpose.

4. I trust God to rebuild my mindset and guide me toward healthy relationship patterns.

5. I choose to see men and women through the lens of God's love and truth.

6. I attract relationships that align with God's will and protect my purpose.

7. I speak life over my future, knowing God's blueprint leads to lasting joy and peace.

8. I am free from my past — I am free to build a beautiful, happy, and healthy marriage.

9. I honor my season of renewal by walking in wisdom, patience, and discernment.

10. I am a wise builder, laying every brick of my future on the solid rock of God's Word.

Chapter 3 Decrees

1. I reject culture's lies and boldly embrace Kingdom truth in my relationships.
2. I build on God's Word, instead of vibes, energy, or shifting emotions.
3. I recognize red flags and refuse to ignore them or make excuses.
4. I am a wise builder who follows God's blueprint for love, connection, and purpose.
5. I value covenant over convenience and purpose over popularity.
6. I resist being swept away by culture's undertow — I stand firm on the Rock of God's truth.
7. I choose honor, trust, and intentionality in every connection I make.
8. I guard my heart and steward my emotions with wisdom and discernment.
9. I let go of false cultural patterns and embrace God's standard for lasting love.
10. I am being transformed daily by the renewing of my mind, and I walk in Kingdom confidence.

Chapter 4 Decrees

1. I am healing deeply and completely through God's love and truth.
2. I resist being led by trauma or pain — I embrace being led by God's purpose and peace.
3. I choose relationships that reflect God's purpose for my life.
4. I am free from emotional bondage and being drawn to dysfunction.
5. I attract healthy love because I value myself the way God values me.
6. I set wise boundaries that protect my heart and preserve my peace.
7. I release old soul ties and replace them with Kingdom alignment.
8. I recognize and reject trauma bonds disguised as love.
9. I trust God to guard my heart and lead me into healthy covenant connection.
10. I love from a whole place, not a hurting one — and my future is secure in Him.

Chapter 5 Decrees

1. My preferences are being purified to align with God's plan for my life and legacy.
2. I am free from trauma bonds — I recognize dysfunction and no longer call it love.
3. I desire what is good, godly, and growth-producing in a relationship.
4. I release bitterness and make room for healing, growth, and joy.
5. I choose to heal, not to harbor pain.
6. I walk in love and mercy without letting past wounds direct my future.
7. I cancel the power of offense over my heart and mind.
8. I trust God to be my defender and restorer.
9. I am being refined by His purpose.
10. I am free — mentally, emotionally, physically, and spiritually — through the power of forgiveness.

Chapter 6 Decrees

1. I am patient and kind, because covenant love refuses to rush or wound.
2. I resist envy or boasting — God's Love Secures me.
3. I humble myself and resist pride, and self-centered thinking.
4. I resist being easily provoked, and allow kindness, and patience to rule my behavior.
5. I resist keeping score of wrongs; I choose forgiveness because love keeps no record of being wronged.
6. I look for the best, believe the best, and hope for the best for people
7. I let go of the need to be pursued by people who are not sent by God.
8. I cooperate with God's love in me that is patient, kind, and enduring.
9. The love I have for others reflects God's heart — It is strong, pure, and faithful.
10. I walk in covenant love that does not fade, and never fails.

Chapter 7 Decrees

1. I honor God with my body, my choices, and my boundaries.
2. I practice sexual sobriety as an act of daily worship and wisdom.
3. My worth supersedes culture, pressure, or past mistakes.
4. I reject compromise and choose covenant purity.
5. I set clear boundaries that protect my heart, mind, and spirit.
6. I am not my own — I was bought with a price, and I honor God with my life.
7. I stand firm on God's truth without conforming to culture's lies.
8. I walk in sexual integrity, accountability, and intentionality.
9. I am preparing for covenant love by living with honor today.
10. I let go of shame, and receive grace, and live as a whole, healed vessel of God.

Chapter 8 Decrees

1. I confront past hurts with without blame, but in faith, and healing abounds in my soul.
2. I humbly forgive and renounce every offense I have taken.
3. I am free from my past — I am who God says I am.
4. I renounce every generational pattern that doesn't align with God's love and purpose for my life.
5. God's will determines my purpose.
6. I am free to love, trust, and connect in healthy, God-honoring ways.
7. God is my perfect Father — He has provided healing through Jesus Christ — I believe and receive it.
8. I choose new patterns that bless my future and my legacy.
9. My heart is open to love without fear because I am fully seen, safe, and secure in Christ.
10. I am the cycle-breaker — through God's truth and grace.

Chapter 9 Decrees

1. I grow best in Godly community — isolation is no longer my safe space.

2. I invite wise, loving accountability into my journey because I was not created to heal alone.

3. I am surrounded by voices that sharpen, not shame me.

4. I reject the lie that privacy equals protection — I choose truth, trust, and transparency.

5. I welcome correction from those anchored in God's Word, because correction brings wisdom.

6. I am open, honest, and accountable with faith-filled mentors who speak life into me.

7. I choose my community based on the God given purpose for my life.

8. My transformation is deepened through connection, not control.

9. I renounce offenses, pride and isolation and I welcome sharpening relationships.

10. God is placing the right people around me to help me grow, stay grounded, and thrive.

Chapter 10 Decrees

1. I trust God's timing over my own because He sees what I cannot see.
2. I am on time — I am in process, and God is preparing me for something great.
3. I release fear and comparison; my path is custom-designed by God.
4. I commit my plans to the Lord, and I trust He will establish every step (Proverbs 16:3).
5. I will remain strong in doing the right thing, for in due season I will reap if I do not give up (Galatians 6:9).
6. God has not forgotten me — He is setting the stage for something better than I imagined.
7. I am using this waiting season to grow, heal, and become ready for what's coming.
8. I will not confuse speed with blessing — I trust that God is both intentional and protective.
9. Delays are not denials — they are divine redirections for my safety and success.
10. My faith is in God's perfect plan, and I choose to wait with purpose, peace, and praise.

Chapter 11 Decrees

1. I am committed to pursuing peace in all situations. (Hebrews 12:14)

2. I trust God to reveal the truth behind charm, chemistry, and conversation.

3. I slow down, seek wise counsel, and observe fruit over time.

4. I am worthy of truth, peace, and alignment.

5. My feelings are real, but God's Word is final.

6. I reject counterfeit connections and make room for God's best.

7. I listen to the Holy Spirit and allow peace to confirm my steps.

8. I walk in wisdom and spiritual clarity.

9. I am a discerning builder, choosing character over hype.

10. I declare Matthew 7:16 over my life — I will know them by their fruit, not their performance.

Chapter 12 Decrees

1. I am whole, healed, and anchored in God's truth.

2. I am actively being prepared and am surrendered and growing.

3. I am no longer waiting to be "fixed" — I am walking in freedom and wholeness now.

4. My identity is secure in Christ and I am prime for a Godly relationship and marriage.

5. I bring peace and purpose into every relationship I enter.

6. I am committed to growth and healing — before and after I say "I do."

7. I build my relationship blueprint on the rock of God's word. (Matthew 7:24)

8. I've renewed my mind, and I walk in God's wisdom, and am free from culture's confusion. (Romans 12:2)

9. I am ready to love, communicate, and lead with grace and strength.

10. I am committed to continued mind renewal so my future marriage will reflect God's glory.

Personal Decrees

Key Terms to Know

Chapter 1
Single With a Goal

Blueprint – The internal set of beliefs, habits, and patterns that guide how you design and approach relationships.

Inner Vows – Personal promises made in response to past hurt, often creating limitations in future relationships

Relational Lens – The perspective through which you interpret and respond to interactions in relationships.

Emotional Residue – Lingering feelings from past experiences that influence current relationship behavior.

Chapter 2
Renewing the Relationship Blueprint

Generalization – A broad, absolute statement formed from limited experience, often untrue in all cases.

Replacement Therapy – Replacing false beliefs with biblical truth to create healthier mindsets.

Arguments of the Soul – Internal debates between God's truth and the lies shaped by wounds or culture.

Biblical Scale – Using Scripture as the standard for weighing thoughts, beliefs, and relationship decisions.

Chapter 3
Culture vs. Kingdom

Vibe-Driven Connection – A relationship formed solely on feelings, chemistry, or appearance.

Undertow Principle – The hidden cultural pull that slowly draws you away from God's truth in relationships.

Kingdom Standard – God's design and values for building relationships.

Sand Foundation – Building on unstable qualities such as looks or temporary excitement, leading to collapse under pressure.

Chapter 4
Wholeness Before Oneness

Kingdom Math – The biblical principle that one whole person plus another whole person equals a unified one.

Fix-It Syndrome – Trying to repair or rescue someone unwilling to heal or change.

Soul Ties – Deep emotional or spiritual bonds that tie and confine you to negative relationships.

Christ-Secured Identity – Confidence and self-worth rooted in relationship with Jesus.

Chapter 5
Purpose Over Preference

Trauma Bond – An emotional attachment rooted in shared pain or dysfunctional patterns.

Purpose Alignment – Matching life and relationship goals to God's will rather than personal comfort.

False Familiarity – Mistaking shared wounds for genuine compatibility.

God-Ordained Partnership – A relationship intentionally formed to fulfill divine purpose.

Chapter 6
Redefining Love, Commitment, Sacrifice and Covenant

Covenant Love – Love based on a God-centered commitment, not just emotion. Love is a Command — not an Emotion.

Emotional Love – Feelings-based affection that can fade when circumstances change.

Linchpin – The central "Factor" (God) that holds a relationship together.

Sacrificial Commitment – Willingness to give for the good of the relationship in obedience to God.

Chapter 7
Boundaries, Purity, and Honor

Sexual Sobriety – A daily commitment to God to maintain self-control and sexual purity as a form of worship to God.

God-Honoring Boundaries – Limits set to protect spiritual, emotional, and physical integrity.

Cultural Compromise – Lowering godly standards to fit societal norms.

Honor Code – A personal standard of treating others and oneself with biblical respect.

Chapter 8
Healing Father and Mother Wounds

Generational Patterns – Behaviors and mindsets passed down through family lines.

Parental Imprint – The deep influence a parent's example leaves on a child's beliefs and habits.

Fear of Abandonment – Anxiety about being left or rejected due to early life experiences.

Over-Performance – Striving excessively to earn love and approval.

Chapter 9
The Power of Accountability and Community

Blind Spots – Weaknesses or issues we cannot see in ourselves without outside input.

Accountability Partner – A trusted person who helps you stay aligned with your values.

Teachable Spirit – Openness to correction and growth.

Faith-Filled Community – A group committed to living by biblical principles and mutual support.

Chapter 10
God's Timing versus Your Timeline

Waiting Season – A time of preparation before stepping into a new relationship or life stage.

Comparison Trap – Measuring your life's progress against others, leading to discouragement.

Preparation Process – The personal and spiritual growth that happens before a promise is fulfilled.

Protective Delay – God's intentional timing to safeguard your heart and future.

Chapter 11
Discerning the Right Relationships

Spiritual Alignment – Agreement in faith, values, and life mission.

Fruit Inspection – Evaluating a person's actions and results to discern character. You know the type of tree by it's fruit.

Holy Spirit Leading – Guidance from God's Spirit in making decisions.

Counterfeit Connection – A relationship that looks right on the surface but doesn't align with God's truth.

Chapter 12
Becoming Marriage Ready

Marriage Readiness – Being emotionally, spiritually, and mentally prepared for covenant marriage. Counting the cost and renewing the mind concerning marriage life.

Vision Casting – Creating a shared plan for your future with biblical values at the core.

Continual Check-In – Regular self and couple accountability and counsel to maintain health in the relationship.

Foundation Building – Establishing stability before entering marriage.

Recommended Resources for Your Journey

These books have shaped my understanding of God's Kingdom, relationships, and purpose. They are powerful tools for mind renewal, spiritual growth, and building a strong foundation for God-centered relationships. I encourage you to add them to your personal library.

I'm a Soul Man
by Dr. James D. Treadwell Jr.

This book will transform the way you think about spiritual warfare in your own mind. Dr. Treadwell masterfully teaches how to identify and dismantle the arguments that oppose God's truth in your life. Every believer — especially those preparing for God-centered relationships — needs these tools.

Scan Here to Get Your Copy

https://amzn.to/47lwaPK

Recommended Resources for Your Journey

Who Am I and Why Am I Here?
by Dr. Bill Hamon

Dr. Hamon unpacks God's original design for man and woman to partner in His purpose, reproduce godly families, and fulfill their Kingdom calling. This book will help you discover your ultimate personal purpose and see how your relationships and family fit into God's greater plan.

Scan Here to Get Your Copy

https://amzn.to/458eMwv

Notes

Notes

Notes

Notes

www.ingramcontent.com/pod-product-compliance
Lightning Source LLC
Chambersburg PA
CBHW071159160426
43196CB00011B/2131